Power Made Perfect?

Power Made Perfect?

Is There a Christian Politics for the Twenty-First Century?

Timothy Sherratt

Foreword by
Stan D. Gaede

CASCADE *Books* · Eugene, Oregon

POWER MADE PERFECT?
Is There a Christian Politics for the Twenty-First Century?

Cascade Books
An Imprint of Wipf and Stock Publishers
199 W. 8th Ave., Suite 3
Eugene, OR 97401

www.wipfandstock.com

PAPERBACK ISBN: 978-1-4982-2594-6
HARDCOVER ISBN: 978-1-4982-2596-0

Cataloguing-in-Publication Data

Sherratt, Timothy

Power made perfect? : is there a christian politics for the twenty-first century? / Timothy Sherratt.

xviii + 132 p. ; 23 cm. Includes bibliographical references and index.

ISBN 978-1-4982-2594-6 (PAPERBACK) | ISBN 978-1-4982-2596-0 (HARDCOVER)

1. Christianity and politics. 2. Christian ethics. 3. Social ethics. I. Title.

BJ1251 S285 2016

Manufactured in the U.S.A.   02/26/2016

To Chris, my wife, and to the memory of our parents, Georgia and Theron, Elizabeth and Charles, with love and gratitude

In the world, the Church can only wield the weapons of the Spirit in all purity; she can only wield them helplessly, namely with the naked help of the Cross; and having thus wielded them, she humbly trusts the issue to God.

—CHARLES MALIK, *CHRIST AND CRISIS*

Contents

Foreword

ONE OF THE BENEFITS of writing a foreword is that at most it serves as an appetizer. If the tome is good—as this one most certainly is—readers will quickly move on to the main course. If not . . . well, one has better things to do. I am encouraged by that since there is very little I can add to the insight and wisdom that the reader will discover in Timothy Sherratt's *Power Made Perfect?* It is a gem waiting to be uncovered. Hopefully very, very soon.

We live in an interesting moment, politically speaking. On the one hand, politics is a topic purposely avoided in a whole range of contexts. Certainly that is the case in many churches, where pastors and leaders don't want to be misunderstood or politically pigeonholed; and parishioners want the Gospel, not a political agenda. But it is also true at lunch with your business partners, or dinner with family and friends you deeply love. A strong political statement is laid on the table, and suddenly no one wants to talk. Or eat! And the amity and fellowship that you had hoped for (and even planned on) is suddenly . . . history.

On the other hand, we are all aware of the potential downside of such avoidance. What if Christians had moved more quickly and forcefully to stem the tide of fascism in Germany? What if William Wilberforce had not pursued the implications of his convictions regarding slavery? And we could all add tenfold to this list, simply recounting our own personal journeys. The political realities before us cannot be avoided regardless of how artful we may be at the task. Nor should they be.

The point is, we are desperately (desperately) in need of a deeper wisdom on this topic. And that is precisely what *Power Made Perfect?* provides. The surprise, however, is that it does so without losing those of us who are most in need of it. Meaning me, of course. It is readable but deep, at the same time. Clear but not without the nuance needed for such a complicated topic. The author has spent a lifetime investigating the political landscape, and yet he never loses the forest for the trees. Best of all, this treatise is profoundly biblical and faithful to the One who calls us to follow him. *Wherever* he leads.

Thanks be to God.

—Stan Gaede

Acknowledgments

I GRATEFULLY ACKNOWLEDGE THE help and encouragement of many friends and colleagues in the writing of this book. To former Gordon College students Jenny Hyde and Casey Smedberg, who read drafts and offered comments and helpful suggestions. To Dr. Stan Gaede, who read early chapters and provided much encouragement in the formative stages. To Jim Skillen, who read the complete draft and made the final version so much better than it would have been—the errors that remain are mine, of course. Everyone ought to have the steady friendship and support that Jim has extended to me in over a quarter of a century. To John Topliff, who helped steer this project to my publishers. To my colleagues in the political science department at Gordon College, Ruth Melkonian, Paul Brink, and Mike Jacobs, and to the blessed memory of David Lumsdaine. To All Saints' Anglican Church in Amesbury, which allowed me to try out ideas in "Adult Ed.," and especially to Dr. Paul Aganski for his friendship and support. To the Breakfast Boys because Christian sensibility is shaped by close acquaintance over many years and yours is the best. To Katie Ells Donworth, who provided calm, organized, and invaluable help, and an editor's eye in preparing the manuscript for submission. And last to my family, near and far, for their love, as we navigate together by the light of Christ.

Introduction

Is *Your* Question Here?

—How can Christian politicians avoid catering to the power brokers and moneylenders, especially if they are not independently wealthy?

—Is it wrong not to resist political power when we know a government action is wrong or sinful?

—How should Christians use political power? God worked through the meek and humble, not the powerful.

EARLY IN THE DEVELOPMENT of this project, I asked the adult Sunday school class at my church to write down the questions that they wished a book on politics would address. What do you need to know? I asked them. What would help you get a better purchase on politics and government? Christian political action in the United States the last thirty and more years has a track record, and has acquired a distinctive "shape." What do you make of it? What concerns does it raise? Does the current state of American politics encourage or discourage you? Does the way Christians have engaged in politics encourage or discourage you? What do you know of Christian political initiatives outside the United States? What could Christianity have to offer to American politics that it does not seem to offer, or to be able to offer?

These were the kinds of prompts I put to the people who came to my class. They, in turn, were not slow to generate questions. The questions came thick and fast, like the three that open this introduction.

The aim of my class was to respond to the members' questions as clearly and helpfully as possible—on a topic that proves frustrating to most, if not all of us who watch as political warfare leads to the government shutting down for nearly three weeks, or as the rollout of an important new law governing health insurance stumbles badly.

Why ask the questions? Two reasons are uppermost for me. One is to invite you, the reader, to ponder the questions *your* Christian neighbors are asking. The other reason is self-referential: at about the same time I taught this class, we interviewed a priest for the position of rector—head pastor, for those who don't use this Anglican title. Well, he told the search committee that he prepared sermons by imagining members of his congregation sitting around the table he wrote at. That way, he explained, he would be more likely to engage each and every one of his parishioners because he would have them in mind as he developed his thoughts. As a teacher myself, I can't think of a better mode of preparation. By the time you have worked your way through the chapters that follow, I hope I will have addressed many of my class's questions, directly or indirectly. And of course I hope that yours will be among them.

My class generated a lot of questions and I offer only a sampling of them here. They wanted to know the best way for Christians to engage politics. The high visibility of the Religious Right and the controversy that follows its campaigns on abortion, stem cell research, or gay marriage, let alone its close ties to the Republican Party, prompted several to ask about better ways to organize, communicate, and represent oneself politically. As one put it, "The Moral Majority approach doesn't seem to be working anymore." They wanted to know what to do when civil law and God's law clash. They were concerned about strategy, especially how to engage a culture not much disposed to listen to Christians' arguments in support of unpopular positions. The ideological divide between Democrats and Republicans raised both strategic and ethical questions about partisanship and bipartisanship—is one or the other more ethically appropriate? Democracy itself posed questions. If we live under democratic rules, one person wanted to know, what is the extent of our obligation to follow the majority's decision when it takes the form of laws? Another asked how much political engagement matters. Still another asked my opinion on those Christians who view politics as chiefly another arena for evangelism. What *are* the proper uses for politics? Last, but not least, several questions related to personal and political conduct. As one of my respondents put it, how is a Christian to balance mercy and justice in issues like illegal immigration or capital punishment? When legislators make laws or judges hands-down decisions, should mercy always trump justice?

Looking over these questions, I find that may be usefully grouped into several categories. Traditional and nontraditional students alike want to know what political engagement from a Christian point of view looks like and what it ought to look like. Is there one right model for doing this, or more than one, and how do you evaluate them? Then they want to know how to be sure that political engagement by Christians will remain focused on, or inspired by, the good news and resist getting distracted or diluted. They want to know if they must, or must not, engage politically. They want to know if it is possible to practice an ethical political engagement in this fallen world. Is it possible to engage politically and still please God? They certainly want to know how to respond to opposition to Christianity in the culture, especially when that opposition shapes the laws they must live under. And of course, they want guidance in response to the contemporary issues of our day.

I have tried to organize this book in a way that will most helpfully engage all of these concerns. Sometimes, the way the book does so sets out a context for grappling with the question rather than giving a direct answer. But often the context is the crucial thing.

In response to the first set of questions, we begin with two big models of Christian political engagement, with enough detail in each description to allow us to get "inside" them, to learn about the challenges they faced, to ponder the achievements and disappointments, and to weigh the pros and cons—and at least to take a stab at the question of whether there are one or many authentic Christian approaches to politics.

The first big model is that of the Christian Right in the United States in the latter part of the last century and the first decade or so of this one. I invite us to consider this as a model in its own right and also as part of the bigger story of how religion and politics ("church and state") have interacted in the American republic and how that relationship has changed in recent decades. The second model is that of the Christian Democratic Union (CDU), the political party founded in Germany immediately after World War II, which still plays a prominent role in German politics today. It's little known by Christians or non-Christians in the United States but its rich history and distinctive approach give us plenty to chew on.

Are these the best or most important models? They are not necessarily either but each has much to teach us. Both are substantial and well-developed and each is different from the other in approach and goals. By showing us what believers have actually done to engage politically, together the two pose a very important question: if we do not choose one of these, then what should replace them? How would one organize for political engagement in different ways, and why? What should these models have achieved that neither succeeded in doing?

The Religious Right and Christian Democracy raise a further question, too. Both were motivated by Christian teachings. But is motivation enough? Which *are* the important teachings for political engagement? Is Christian ethics to be the point of departure for Christian politics? I take this up in the third chapter and argue that Christian ethics should not be the starting point for political engagement. Instead we should start from our Easter hope that "Christ is risen!" Here is the lodestar, the guiding principle of the Christian faith, from which Christians take their bearings and draw their encouragement. For this hope, brother and sister Christians have taken up their own crosses, witnessed, served others, suffered, and died. Nor is this confined to the past as Christians in many societies, especially along the fault lines where Christianity and Islam come into contact, continue to face similar challenges. Many others have not lived such spectacular lives. Instead, they have made their lunches and gone to work, as it were, and have worked well, faithfully, and invisibly. But their inspiration has been one and the same.

The Jesus who rose from the dead is also the rightful King—over the entire creation. Here we meet the most important of political realities. It applies to human political authorities of all kinds, democrats as well as dictators. If Christ is King, then *his model, not Caesar's or the one worked out by the American framers',* is the archetype for the exercise of power. We really have to think about this! For democratic and nondemocratic leaders alike, their exercise of power is to be judged against Jesus' standard, not the other way round. And as we come to terms with such a radical (re)understanding of sovereignty, we will meet political power as we have never met it before. How so? Well, the crucifixion was not a divine mistake, a hiccup on the way to restoring God's power over creation after Adam's rebellion. No, the most powerful act of this rightful King was to be put to death by the occupying Romans! Properly understood, power is more closely associated with sacrifice, service, humility, love, and care than with force, will, rights, and conquest. Power is made perfect in weakness.

Such a radical rethinking of rightful power makes urgent an already pressing concern for Christians. How do we please God? For some Protestant denominations, this is a close relative of the question, "How do I know I am saved?" and those denominations have developed a strong tradition of personal holiness, or piety. Political engagement has often been a casualty of an emphasis on personal holiness. We will examine the relationship between pleasing God and political engagement in light of the power made perfect in weakness, and will conclude that piety has a social dimension as well as a personal one. This is the place for a discussion of Christian ethics.

You may want to say at this point, "Oh, I understand that Jesus turned the world upside down by dying for our sins. I understand that he challenges all human political pretensions. But the heights to which he raises the bar are so high and unreachable in this world that I just have to look elsewhere to figure out how ordinary, fallen people should act—in my ordinary, fallen life for starters, let alone the political arena." This is a pivotal point. It is a point about prudence and we consider, in a following chapter, how we should balance Christian ethical principles with real-world circumstances. After all, this is not an occasional dilemma a Christian faces once in a blue moon. It is a permanent one in a fallen world, no less for political than for personal decisions.

Like piety, prudence is also situated at the center of an entire tradition of Christian reflection, including reflection on politics. Some of the very best Christian minds, from St. Augustine to Reinhold Niebuhr, take the tension between biblical principles and human circumstances as the starting point for the entire Christian ethical undertaking. We can only address how to please God or how to craft organized ways of pleasing God in the family, the church, the workplace, or the public square, if we also give due weight to sin. Reinhold Niebuhr warned that pessimism over sin led to ethical complacency, while undue optimism about human potential led to sentimentality—both outcomes to be avoided! So prudence, too, must be part of our conversation about the possibility of a Christian politics.

What the reader will have in his or her possession at this point in the book is a composite Christian perspective drawn from the main traditions of Christian political reflection and organization. I hope to show that all of them, crafting biblically based models for political engagement, pleasing God and acting prudently deserve being taken up together, not separately, and never in separate "camps." Acting prudently *is* a matter of pleasing

God; piety *does* call for faithful application of biblical principles to public policy, and so on.

With the composite perspective in hand, so to speak, three "application" chapters apply it to six issues of contemporary importance in American politics. I selected them for the range of their responsiveness to this Christian perspective and the resulting ethical and strategic challenges they issue to Christians organizing for political service. Of course, six issues, however important they may be, do not make for a comprehensive treatment of America's political challenges, and I make no claim to offer one. But I hope the approach I take will have a wider application.

Is there a Christian politics for this century, as my subtitle has it? There remains a final piece to the puzzle that question poses. The closing chapter tries to supply it by urging believers to "be the church!" Government serves this world, the glorious but fallen creation. The church stands at the juncture of creation and the new creation. It plays a vital role in helping Christians understand their citizenship in the kingdom of God and how they can best live in the fallen world. It helps them take the measure of government purposes and their own responsibilities as citizens. Just as the power of God is made perfect in weakness, so, too, the surprising reality of the church is that it can help us participate in that power, in worship, fellowship, and service.

Is *your* question here?

Chapter 1 _____

Is *That* What You Mean by Christian Politics?

The Religious Right in the United States

BORN AGAIN. HOW QUICKLY we forget that some of the early stirrings of what came to be called the Religious Right stirred first in the Democratic Party. Georgia governor Jimmy Carter became the first self-proclaimed "born-again" president, the first evangelical in the contemporary mold to hold that office. To be sure, the born-again credentials did not keep the evangelical vote in the Democrats' camp for long. Once fellow evangelicals found the President unwilling to embrace publicly their emerging pro-life agenda, their allegiances switched. Within a few short years, today's political alignment was largely in place and *Roe v. Wade* had assumed its role as traffic cop, pointing supporters and opponents to their respective poles—and polls.

As its non-obvious beginnings suggest, there is more complexity to the Religious Right than meets the eye. When evangelicals abandoned Carter they did not join an already socially conservative Republican Party. Far from it. The GOP was the party of business, and had locked itself into what seemed like permanent minority status. To a significant extent, the Republicans' contemporary social conservative identity, stillborn in the anti-communist foreign policy incarnation of Senator Barry Goldwater, came into being as apolitical evangelical Christian citizens sought political shelter in what their leaders told them was a severe moral crisis. For their part, Republican leaders in the mold of Ronald Reagan recognized that social conservatives had flung them an electoral lifeline. They grabbed it and started pulling, all the way to the White House.

The rise of the Religious Right does not, of course, tell anything like the whole story of Christian political initiatives in this country even if we keep to a contemporary time frame. It describes a controversial model of political engagement that has been at the center of important social and cultural changes since the 1970s, though not always on the winning side. For our purposes, the Religious Right provides us a major example of Christian political engagement with enough of a lifespan to show how it has worked and not worked. It has accumulated a record of achievements, forged alliances, and attracted criticisms. Whatever we make of it, we can at least make reliable, evidence-driven judgments about it. In other words, it provides us enough accumulated evidence to ask a very important question: is *that* what is meant by Christian politics?

The story of the Religious Right is best understood as one chapter in a much larger narrative, the story of the relationship between Christianity and democracy in America. Relations between "church and state," which had been impressively stable for the first century and a half of the republic's existence, began to change in the middle of the last century and helped create the conditions under which the Religious Right identified what it saw as the challenges that compelled it to launch its political initiatives.

That larger story, then, must come first.

Christianity and American Democracy: Marriage, Separation, and Finger-Pointing

The story of Christianity and democracy in America[1] resembles an arranged marriage that served both partners well but eventually unraveled. It was a curious marriage since the spouses spent little time together and occupied separate bedrooms. Now ex-spouses, but remaining in the same town and knowing the same people, each tells self-serving and unflattering stories about the other and neither is willing to give much ground. For this is not just a story about church-state relations. It is also the story of the ideological polarization that infects American politics in our own day.

The framers of the Constitution arranged the marriage in the first place. Hugh Heclo dubs it "The Great Denouement," and he describes it as a sort of peace treaty that launched the new republic in a direction that led away from Europe's religious wars. The pact secured individual freedom of religious conscience and was preserved by separating the structures

---

1. I am relying heavily on certain sources for this account, chiefly on Hugh Heclo's *Christianity and American Democracy*. Avoiding the common analytical trap of addressing "religion" in general, rather than Christianity in particular, Heclo manages to keep his analysis focused and precise, and the results are insightful.

Christianity and democracy respectively inhabited. "The practical political effect," Heclo says, "was to house-train an issue drenched in centuries of blood and turn it into something ordinary people could live with—indeed, participate in—amid relative peace."[2]

The Constitution set out the terms of the marriage. The two spouses were given distinct and separate roles to play. Three brief clauses were all that was necessary. In Article VI of the original document, religious tests for holding federal office were prohibited. In the First Amendment, Congress was instructed not to interfere with religious establishments and not to obstruct the "free exercise" of religion. In plain language, there was to be no religious discrimination or favoritism of the kind that said, "No Catholics for President," or "Only card-carrying, fully immersed Baptists for Congress." Free exercise established a right for citizens to practice religion as they wished. By separating church and state, it became possible for religion and democracy to actually become partners, to work in complementary ways and not in competition for power.

The wording of the so-called "Establishment Clause" of the First Amendment suggests that the framers never considered that separation had to be absolute. To be sure, the clause has developed into a wide and high barrier against all sorts of government activity—government-sponsored prayers in schools, taxes supporting creeds one does not accept, and so forth. But that came largely in the twentieth century. At its adoption, the Establishment Clause seems to have had a different intent altogether. The clause is brief: "Congress shall make no law respecting an establishment of religion." At the time, several states *had* establishments that gave tax support to particular denominations. Massachusetts was one of these, the Congregational Church being the beneficiary. And it retained that benefit until 1833.

In 1787, ratification of the new Constitution was not a sure thing. "Anti-Federalists" feared the powers of the new federal government and worked against ratification. The Bill of Rights, containing the First Amendment, which in turn contains the Establishment Clause, reassured the states that the federal government would not trample on their practices, including establishment. Regulation of religion rested with the states.

But in time, the remaining establishments were abandoned and forgotten. By the mid-twentieth century, courts were ready to read fresh meaning into the phrase "establishment of religion." But before we get to that part of

2. Ibid., 73.

the story, let's pause to acknowledge the remarkable achievement crafted by the Constitution's framers.

They got along, Christianity and democracy, for more than a century, providing each other with valuable mutual benefits. Christianity gave purpose and legitimacy to American democratic government. Despite having no official status, religion provided the new republic a shared Protestant language, culture, and morality. This would prove helpful because a political system that was federal (possessing two levels of government), democratic (promoting majority rule), and liberal (oriented toward individual rights) contained centrifugal forces capable of undermining the hoped-for unity of the new nation. A common Protestant culture balanced these forces and worked to integrate society. Even revivalism and the do-good impulses of Christian morality "opened up new spaces in political society that women and other oppressed groups had never had access to before."[3] Finally, the mere flourishing of religious groups, especially Protestant ones with their theology of the immanence of Christ and their grassroots organizing provided "schools for democracy." In real and practical ways, churches cultivated the skills and attitudes helpful to running a democratically organized political system.

Democracy gave American religion a context for and a need to get along with other religions and a need to accommodate its own multiple expressions. It validated denominations and a kind of religious pluralism. Religion could flourish because no one denomination would run into official restrictions, nor would the various sects have to compete against officially favored competitors.

Democracy's influence was not entirely benign. Heclo has it encouraging an "open market religious competition" among denominations for converts, one that fostered a "quite un-Christian idea of historical progress."[4] A democratic spirit pushed religious leaders to cherry pick democratic norms from the Scriptures to demonstrate just how friendly Christianity was to a culture of choice and equality. As Heclo points out, this tendency struck at the core of Christianity's message—Christ is risen—distorting or obscuring the supernatural character of the faith.

While these tendencies persisted—both those that led to bad habits and those that led to good ones—the marriage remained secure for many decades. It unraveled little by little. A string of legal decisions, culminating

3. Ibid., 73–74.
4. Ibid., 44–45.

in the 1960s decisions banning prayer in public schools, reworked the loose relationship between church and state into one that insisted on the "strict separation" of the two. What had been originally intended to prevent the federal government from interfering with a state's establishment now became a full-fledged *individual* right not to be established against. The new position held that religion should remain strictly private and was not to "touch" government or politics in any way.

Christian denominations displayed a wide range of responses to these developments. The old mainline churches—Episcopalians, Methodists, and Presbyterians—were more inclined to see such matters through the prism of civil rights rather than biblical teachings. When viewed from the civil rights perspective, abortion rights advanced the cause of women, extending to them control over their lives. Roman Catholics, only recently encouraged by the Second Vatican Council (1962–1965) to participate fully in church life, and by the election of John F. Kennedy to see themselves no longer as immigrants but as full-fledged citizens, came to the abortion debate with well-formed teachings. In due course, conservative Catholics organized robust opposition and exercised broad influence. But many of their number were still tied by class, sympathy, and history to Roosevelt's New Deal and its expanded version launched by Lyndon Johnson as the Great Society. Their politics were Democratic and their instinctive response to social legislation was to attempt change from within. Although this was soon relegated to a rearguard action in the face of the strong progressive bent the Democratic Party developed, some prominent Catholics carved out a distinctive position and tried hard to hold on to it. This position, upheld by Sargent Shriver in the Kennedy-Johnson years and Governor Robert Casey in the 1990s, embraced a large social safety net and upheld the "culture of life," that is, an emphatically pro-life position on abortion.

Evangelical and fundamentalist Protestants responded to the school prayer and abortion rulings with a mixture of alarm and guilt—eventually. As Randall Balmer has pointed out, they had paid relatively little attention to abortion and did not have a well-developed position on the question in the early 1970s.[5] Leaders had to first articulate the importance of the issue from a Christian perspective. For decades, the social and political presence of many Christians of these persuasions had been minimal. Now, old assumptions that America retained a basically Christian national culture were shattered. Fundamentalists and evangelicals knew very few formers

---

5. Balmer, "The Real Origins of the Religious Right."

and shapers of politics and culture. Their first spokespeople were in the Bryan tradition—preachers, like Jerry Falwell, with a distinctly populist tone to their oratory—not politicians, and they learned politics from the outside and only by making some mistakes. They rejected abortion under almost all circumstances. And they read into its 1973 validation as an individual right a cultural revolution all the more devastating for emerging by stealth. Casting around for language to make sense of this, they resorted first to religious rather than political terminology, christening the revolution as one guided by secular humanism. In time, more prosaic and more political terms would emerge, with "liberal" the most widely employed.

Like most Catholics, evangelicals in the emerging Religious Right also had a Democrat past. Many were Southerners in the conservative wing of a party that had turned sharply away from segregation. Others inherited the tradition of William Jennings Bryan's nineteenth-century populism and their parents' generation had followed Bryan into cultural exile after the Scopes Trial of 1925.

Southern conservatives who were also evangelical Protestants did not immediately depart from the party or see the GOP as the logical place to take their stand. Many hoped, logically enough, to reassert the conservatism of their own party, to which they had given unstinting loyalty since Reconstruction. Remember, the first "born-again" president was no Republican—although to be sure, he was not a particularly conservative Southern Democrat either—Governor Jimmy Carter of Georgia.

If the movement took some time to sort itself out, the political parties also took some time to comprehend what sort of cultural movement had been launched. Not until the 1980s were the lines of political allegiance drawn in ways that look familiar to us today. Much is owed to Republican strategists for the allegiances that did finally emerge. The Reagan campaign essentially "converted" Southern segregationists into "traditional values Christians," appealing to their concerns over abortion, prayer, and civil rights to drive a wedge between them and their old affiliation with the Democratic Party. These strategists portrayed the Democratic Party as out of touch with its own grassroots, forcing an unwelcome social agenda on ordinary Americans. This was the "tax and spend" party of the "big government" that the Great Society programs represented. The latter strategy was calculated to play off the several interconnected themes—political, sociological, and religious—in the old South. Suspicion of the federal government, social conservatism, and rejection of redistributive policies that ran contrary to the Protestant ethic of individual effort and reward reinforced one another. It was a highly effective strategy that also capitalized on the weakness of the Carter presidency and the extraordinary popular appeal of Ronald Reagan. In a political sea change, the old "Solid South" abandoned the Democrats and became as solidly supportive of the Republicans. In 1988, the Democratic candidate, Governor Michael Dukakis of Massachusetts, won no electoral votes at all south of the Mason-Dixon Line.

Six of One, Half a Dozen of the Other . . .

To sample media coverage of today's toxic American political climate, one could be tempted to draw the conclusion that on one side lies raging irrationality, while on the other all is sweetness and light. The Tea Party, "extremists," and social and religious conservatives are collectively labeled "unreasonable" and "unwilling to compromise." One step up from popular media, two respected congressional scholars, leading their readers to the conclusion that *It's Even Worse Than It Looks*,[6] disproportionately blamed Republicans and their surrogates for contemporary political woes during the first Obama administration.

That is only half of the story, however. This chapter is both about the rise of the Religious Right and about the political climate it helped to create. There were always two partners in the marriage of Christianity and American democracy and it's time to address the second of these.

Liberal democracy is both of recent and ancient origin. In the language of America's philosophical pedigree, the "liberal" element refers to the tradition of natural rights. This philosophical tradition has shown extraordinary staying power in American life and culture, largely because it supplied the Revolution with its justifying arguments and because it lives on in the Bill of Rights—it's written into our constitution so the courts come back to it again and again to resolve challenges to laws. In the Declaration of Independence it supplied the rationale that interpreted the various actions of successive British governments toward the American colonies as the worst of political crimes—tyranny. What the tyrant had done—what made him a tyrant—was to abuse the rights of life, liberty, and property of the American colonists, imposing taxes and other obligations on them without their consent. Viewed through the lens of a philosophy that made

6. Mann and Ornstein, *It's Even Worse Than It Looks*.

consent basic to the legitimacy of government, the actions of the British government failed every test.

The language of individual rights and consent of the governed, sometimes collectively referred to as the "social contract," exercises influence far beyond its eighteenth-century popularity as philosophical fashion because so much of it made its way into the Bill of Rights. Its language and logic is the official language and logic for resolving disputes between citizens and government. The eventual abolition of slavery after the Civil War further strengthened its role in public life. The Fourteenth Amendment of 1868 deployed that same language to strengthen citizens' rights to life, liberty, property, and—a very significant expansion—equal protection under the law.

In something like the same way that *Roe v. Wade* galvanized the uncompromising style of the Religious Right, the civil rights movement did for the uncompromising style of contemporary liberalism. The renewed emphasis on individual rights made the modern civil rights movement possible, but individual rights did not make the leap to absolute status all at once. To begin with, the most eloquent arguments for civil rights drew from an explicitly Christian characterization of justice and human dignity. In his famous *Letter from Birmingham Jail,* the Rev. Martin Luther King Jr. spoke of rights in the context of justice and of justice in the context of God's law. King wrote, "A just law is a man-made code that squares with the moral law or the law of God. An unjust law is a code that is out of harmony with the moral law." King also invoked "an inescapable network of mutuality" in support of nonviolent resistance to segregation laws. That was the point of his writing to the white ministers of Birmingham. As members of society, and especially as members of the body of Christ, they had an obligation to address injustice.

As *Letter from Birmingham Jail* shows, the Christian argument for justice and the liberal argument for rights maintained harmony in 1963. But the subsequent deployment of rights to justify an enlarged view of government responsibilities suggests that this harmony was more apparent than real. Ironically, those who embraced a progressive view of politics without regard to the Christian moral code found in the civil rights movement a general justification for government intervention. If government *must* act to redress these violations of basic human rights as a moral responsibility, then its responsibility might extend to other kinds of violations as well. This was an important impetus behind the 1960s War on Poverty. Jim Crow segregation had been enshrined in the legal code, enacted as law. But hadn't government's economic decision-making also created a system of laws and couldn't poverty be linked to that system's functioning? Here, too, one could argue—and many did—that the system was to blame. So, the same moral pressure was brought to bear, obliging government to respond as the responsible agent.[7] Expanding government's responsibility for economic outcomes by lending it the moral fervor associated with civil rights made the recipients of welfare the possessors of something very like basic rights.[8]

There is much irony to these developments. If the Christian moral code had been set aside in favor of the obligations generated by rights alone, its influence persisted in the decidedly moralistic tone of the replacement. Perhaps the Progressive apple did not fall far from the Puritan tree!

If the civil rights movement puts the spotlight on the marriage between Christianity and democracy on the brink of its dissolution, the divorce has given the natural rights tradition something it still lacked even though it has long been firmly entrenched in constitutional and legal thinking. Now it gained an independence it had not enjoyed since the American Revolution was harnessed to its ideals. As already observed, the Protestant culture once supplied American democracy with a common moral code, the more useful for being all but universal. But evangelical Protestant political activism in the wake of *Roe v. Wade* exposed cracks in the supposed unity of American Christianity because it attached Christianity to political positions and party allegiances that called its political neutrality into question. That neutrality had been vital to the legitimacy and wide appeal of the Protestant moral code. In the very process of mounting a campaign to secure traditional values, the campaigners unintentionally threw tradition and neutrality aside and made their case much harder to sustain.

So it is not surprising that in the last few decades, liberal democracy has reasserted itself independently of any Christian ethical anchor as the processes described by Hugh Heclo have made themselves felt. Quite

7. This was not the first time that similar ideas had been floated. President Franklin Roosevelt, in his 1944 State of the Union address, proposed an Economic Bill of Rights beginning with a right to employment at a living wage and extending through a lengthy list that included such items as the right of every family to a "decent home." The idea that these could be enshrined as constitutional guarantees that obliged government to secure them is breathtaking in its conceit, and challenges the imagination to grapple with the necessary size, scope, and raw power of that government.

8. It is important to note that, although quasi-rights language—"entitlements," most obviously—pervaded 1960s welfare legislation, these referred strictly speaking to meeting the qualifications for means-based welfare distribution, not to legal or constitutional rights per se.

quickly in cultural development terms, natural rights have become the new moral absolutes. When the old Protestant culture supplied society's moral moorings, natural rights did not, and did not need to, play this role. Now, in the hostile atmosphere created by the abortion decision, liberal democracy voiced the view that Christianity was a repository of reactionary values and obligations, intolerant of choice, and hostile to freedom and equality. Sectarian views should be respected, liberalism argued, but their reach should be confined to the sectarians who held them. Returning the favor, some evangelical and fundamentalist Christians voiced dire warnings of the general collapse of American morals, characterized liberal democracy as an alien philosophy of secular humanism, and stressed its abandonment of traditional, i.e. Christian, moral norms.

As I have suggested, what lends these developments extra-political and cultural significance is the affiliation of Christianity and democracy with the Republican and Democratic parties respectively. Evangelical Christians could have rebuilt allegiance with the Democratic Party, especially if President Carter had taken socially conservative positions on issues like abortion. But it was not to be. Instead, the Democratic Party took on a more liberal cast as its socially conservative members departed. In turn, the GOP acquired a socially conservative wing, one that would lend considerable support to the party for decades to come.

It wasn't just a matter of subtracting social conservatives from one party and adding them to the other, however. The process also made each party more homogeneous, lodging its center further to the left or right respectively. With each successive election, the Republicans became more conservative, the Democrats more liberal.

Evangelical Protestantism and progressive liberalism might have played influential roles in the politics of the last few decades without those roles becoming the major fault line in American politics. But once they had begun to operate through separate political parties—not a foregone conclusion as I have been at pains to point out—the stage was set for today's ideological conflict. Basic beliefs, one could say, are now nearer the surface of American politics than ever before. On the Republican side, core religious principles shaped uncompromising attitudes chiefly on the social issues at first. But soon the same attitude elevated other issues—the free market is the leading candidate—to similar "fundamental moral fact" status. On the Democratic side, rights in general (but equality in particular) came to enjoy an equivalent prestige and levels of support.

The Religious Right: Goals, Methods, and Leadership

The Religious Right addressed politics by developing the political organizations its leaders thought worked best. To use political science terms, a series of interest groups emerged to build up membership and to lobby government for changes in policy.

Representative groups included the National Right to Life Committee, the Moral Majority, Focus on the Family, the Christian Coalition, the Family Research Council, and the Christian Broadcasting Network. Of those organizations, the earlier ones rallied supporters first and engaged issues as a second order of priority. But with the Christian Coalition, founded by CBN founder Pat Robertson and administered by Ralph Reed, the Religious Right moved into electoral politics in an organized and effective fashion. Their biggest coup, and the one that assured Republicans of the political influence of their social conservative bloc, was the sixty-seat shift in the composition of the House of Representatives in the 1994 midterm elections. The result was a Republican takeover after forty years as the minority party.

The value of the association with—one could refer to colonization of—the Republican Party for organizations with the interests of the Religious Right comes into focus when supportive administrations take office. The filling of cabinet portfolios and the nomination of new Supreme Court justices and other federal judgeships, can all reflect the kind of philosophical considerations to which the Religious Right is sensitive. Similarly, party politics allows the various organizations to seek funding and new members whether they win or lose. If they win, the process is vindicated in the good relations and open doors that a favorable administration can foster. If they lose, they draw their members into the adversarial system to warn of the dire consequences that follow from defeat.

The Religious Right's goals are as disparate as those of the organizations that comprise it. They include among other things opposition to abortion, support for religious liberty, opposition to obtaining stem cells from human embryos, and opposition to gay marriage.

Besides party politics, lobbying, and broadcasting, the organizational means employed by the Religious Right are significant in the field of education. Here, evangelicals dominate the homeschool movement, with some 80 percent of homeschoolers identifying with evangelicalism. In higher education, Liberty University, Regent University, and Patrick Henry College have strong links with the Religious Right.

The term *Religious Right* is at best a label of convenience. To employ more precise language risks lopping off significant supporters. So, *evangelical* or even *Christian*, though used often enough, are narrower definitions and imply a precision that may not exist. Even so, evangelical Christians remain at the core of the Religious Right's activism, even if the older, and in a sense founding, generation is now dying off.

The American Religious Right has found most of its unity in ideological agreement rather than strong leadership. Conservative movements generally, including the more recent Tea Party movements, have resisted being organized into larger causes, and have been especially resistant to politicians eager to claim the leadership moniker. For example, despite her rise to prominence after the 2008 elections, former Alaska governor Sarah Palin failed in her bid to be recognized as that leader. There are limits, accordingly, to the degree of agreement that the Religious Right can achieve. At the same time, its decentralized character, the fact that it puts down roots in broadcasting, homeschooling, religious higher education, and interest group lobbying speaks to a movement that will not be overturned by any single set of political developments. The decentralized American political system can deny a party the executive branch without reducing its power and influence to any significant extent, as the years of divided government make plain.

The Religious Right has endured successfully, if consistent commitment to its positions is taken as the measure of success. Whether that is a reflection of reluctance to engage in pragmatic politics or a reflection of the strength of religious commitment in American society, the Religious Right has remained uncompromising in its opposition to abortion and same-sex marriage. As noted earlier, this level of commitment has drawn other issues into its orbit and it has treated these as deserving the same level of commitment. Hostility toward big government and support for the free market both fall into this category. To some extent, of course, the Religious Right's persistence may reflect the slower pace of secularization in American, as opposed to European, society. It has not been necessary to soft-pedal either the message or the style of its delivery. What the Religious Right has acquired is more political know-how and a more sophisticated appreciation of the workings of party politics.

Conclusion

Fifteen years into the present century, the Religious Right appears as steadfast as ever, but its uncompromising political style has earned it many enemies. The mutual hostility between Christianity and democracy continues to play out in party politics and shows few signs of abating.

Christian scholars in the United States have expressed a range of concerns at this situation. Some, like Hugh Heclo, have anticipated a future in which Christianity is placed under considerable pressure to exit the political and legal arena. Others, like David Gushee,[9] have attempted to develop an evangelical center as a rallying place for evangelicals who distance themselves from Religious Right goals and methods. An older evangelical Left, represented by prominent leaders like Jim Wallis, has enjoyed some prominence in election politics in the last decade or so. Still others, prominent among them James Davison Hunter, have called for a pause to give time for reorientation of the "Christian politics" project. Hunter advises a posture of what he terms Faithful Presence to replace the political activism of the last several decades, which he regards as minimally effective in securing policy goals, mistaken in its bottom-up efforts to transform culture from the grassroots, and unfortunate in its distortion of the Christian gospel. Faithful Presence is a call for Christians to practice the faith sincerely and throughout society, in organized but not overtly aggressive ways.

That part of Hunter's advice that involves rethinking the project of Christian political engagement from the ground up will be our focus later in the book. But now it's time to examine a second "big model" of Christian engagement, with an even lengthier pedigree than the Religious Right and a very different style, tone, and approach to politics. Lengthy pedigree or no, it's little known in the United States. It's time to examine Christian Democracy.

9. See Gushee, *The Future of Faith in American Politics.*

Chapter 2 _____

Or *This?*

Christian Democracy in Germany

In 1945, Germany lay in ruins and its cities under Allied occupation. Konrad Adenauer was a fortunate survivor. The long-time mayor of Cologne in the 1920s and early 1930s, he had been a pillar of the Catholic Center Party, which represented an early model of Christian political organizing launched in the previous century. The rise of the Nazis had taken Adenauer and his party by surprise, as indeed it had taken so many others by surprise. Since 1935 he had lived almost in exile, under police observation and legal suspicion. Marked down for elimination, he had been lucky to escape with his life when the Gestapo, who had investigated him for possible ties to the 1944 plot to assassinate Hitler, found the Nazi infrastructure collapsing around them in the final few months of the war, and so were unable to carry out plans to have him killed.[1]

An observant Roman Catholic, Adenauer had spent some of his exile at a Benedictine abbey. There he read *Rerum Novarum* and *Quadragesimo Anno,* the two great Catholic social encyclicals of 1891 and 1931 respectively, which addressed the tasks and limits of government in relation to the rights and needs of society and its members. Although he had been raised in a devout Catholic home and instilled a similar devotion in his own family, Adenauer's politics and his Catholicism were now brought into a new relationship. Adenauer's Catholic insights into the political order could not bear fruit for more than a decade. Not until the war had ended did he reenter politics, and then only to be dismissed by the British occupation forces, who alleged his incompetence in the reconstruction of Cologne! Despite this setback, he helped found a new political party, the Christian

---

1. The two major sources I have relied on for this summary of Christian Democratic politics in Germany are: Williams, *Adenauer,* and Cary, *The Path to Christian Democracy.*

Democratic Union (CDU), and, due as much to his ruthless political skill as to his eloquence or his faith convictions, duly became the first chancellor of the new Federal Republic of West Germany.

Adenauer held the chancellorship for the next seventeen years. That was an extraordinary achievement in itself, not least because he took office when he was already sixty-eight years old. But during that time, the creation and preservation of West Germany against a host of internal and external threats was his constant aim. In some respects he failed, most notably in his inability to prevent the establishment of East Germany, under Soviet influence, as a separate nation-state. But he was successful in reintegrating the Saar region (a German territory on the border with France and occupied by France at the end of the war) into the federal republic as a new province (or state), and presided over the extraordinary economic growth that Germany enjoyed throughout the 1950s.

Even the division of Germany into two states proved to be an opportunity as much as a setback. Adenauer used East Germany's Soviet satellite status to paint the main opposition party in West Germany, the Social Democrats (SDP), as shills for the Soviets and thus unqualified to serve as Germany's loyal opposition, let alone as a governing party. So relentless and effective was this strategy that in 1959 the Social Democrats officially foreswore Marxism and embraced capitalism to make themselves more acceptable to German voters.

It would be contrary to the evidence to assert that the insights gleaned from those papal encyclicals that Adenauer read in exile in the 1930s played a dominant role in all these Cold War political machinations, let alone an exclusive one that pushed other considerations to the margins. Certainly, the Cold War was crystallized in his imagination as waged by godless totalitarianism against the Judeo-Christian civilization of the West, and no doubt this was due in some part to this encounter among other powerful influences.

In practical terms, Adenauer calculated that West Germany's future was tied to the need for a stable western Europe, and a stable western Europe depended on stable Franco-German relations. Three major wars since the 1870s, the last two especially devastating, had made the French deeply suspicious of German intentions. To provide the beginnings of reconciliation, Adenauer joined forces with French ministers Robert Schuman and Jean Monnet to place coal mining and steel production in the two nations under the direction of a new body, the European Coal and Steel Federation. Coal and steel production, it was reasoned, were essential to the armaments industry, so their removal from control by the governments of France and Germany and their relocation to this new governing body significantly limited the threat of a revived arms race between France and Germany. Moreover, it enabled the two nations to view the coal-rich Saar region less as a border region laden with military significance—France occupied the region following both the First and the Second World Wars—and more as a significant source of Europe's industrial stability. In due course the Saar reentered the German Federal Republic. The Coal and Steel Federation represented the embryonic stage of what would become the European Union.

These developments led to a more far-reaching initiative to forge closer economic and political ties across much of western Europe, and at the Treaty of Rome in 1957, six western European nations launched a federal union. Significantly, the underlying rationale for this union was the Catholic principle of *subsidiarity*, which had found its fullest expression in *Quadragesimo Anno* of 1931—one of the encyclicals Adenauer studied during his monastic sojourn. Subsidiarity is a nuanced principle, which has its origin in God's designating Adam to have dominion over all creation as its steward. The logic of the principle holds that stewardship has several dimensions. Representative examples include agriculture, parenting, wealth generation, and the administration of justice. As reflections of God's will, human responsibilities are unique and necessary and so are those institutions formed to carry them out. Responsibilities cannot simply be switched from one agency to another. Governments make bad parents but good dispensers of justice; family relations are inappropriate for running business enterprises, and so on.

Human beings require both opportunity and means to carry out their responsibilities, which in political terms are usually accomplished by erecting protective barriers to government interference with personal choice and empowering government to foster the healthy functioning of society within the limitations just referred to. The principle of subsidiarity holds that no single human agency, especially government, can claim to be all-competent. The popes, especially John Paul II, have held the claim to all-encompassing competence to be the central error of the communist regimes.

These examples focus on the Catholic principle of subsidiarity. That principle provides guidance as to the division of responsibility between governmental and nongovernmental institutions. Its relevance to the thinking behind the European Union lay in its analogous application to various *levels* of government. As we have seen, the European Coal and Steel

Federation took supervision of those core industries out of the hands of national governments. A near equivalent in the United States would be the transfer of a function from state governments to the federal government, such as occurred when the American Constitution was drawn up. Prior to the Federal Convention, for example, states operated with the kind of independence that nation-states usually enjoy, minting their own currencies and entering into formal relations with foreign states. By the terms of the Constitution, both these practices were forbidden and the power was lodged exclusively in the federal government.

By the Treaty of Rome (1957), the new European federal union began the task of identifying other functions beyond those basic extractive industries that would be better administered by European bodies than by national governments.

Adenauer's Christian Democratic Union (CDU) flourished in the Cold War, as did Christian Democrat parties in other European countries, as the principal alternative to European socialist and social democratic parties and their policies. For this reason, the adjective "Christian" has been treated as adding very little to essentially conservative, anti-socialist political movements. Such a definition won't stand up under the weight of the evidence, however. To be sure, Christian Democracy draws on what were widely held principles of human dignity and takes a traditional approach to family life. It views parenting as an aspect of stewardship, as we saw above, and regards the family as a God-given and ultimately irreplaceable institution. In this respect, the Christian-Democracy-just-means-conservative thesis holds up reasonably well.

The same principles underwrote Christian Democrat economic policies, however. Here Christian Democracy defies the conventional categories, such as liberal, socialist, or conservative. Christian Democrat economic policies combined strong support for private enterprise with a commitment to reconciliation among social classes. American readers may need to recall that class-based theories of society permeated most European societies, even as these societies had transformed their political systems into systems of constitutional democracy over the previous century. Class divisions and thus class conflict remained as a major influence on political affiliations. For a political party to declare itself committed to reconciliation *across* social classes risked alienating the traditional supporters of each of those classes, support conditioned to view other classes with suspicion as competitors.

Adenauer's party made this policy of reconciliation work in several ways. These included support for unions, and for collective bargaining agreements, and the creation of a sizeable social safety net. Evidently, this mix of policies and values cannot be forced into a mold labeled simply "conservative." Instead, it represents an interesting combination of the highly principled—for reconciliation is a core Christian principle—and the pragmatic, because these agreements, usually termed "social capitalism" helped secure for postwar West Germany the kind of labor-management peace that helped fuel the so-called economic miracle of rapid rebuilding and economic growth after 1945.

Christian Democracy has not remained stagnant. It remains common to see the leaders of Christian Democrat parties occupying high office—Chancellor Angela Merkel, reelected in 2013 to a third term, is the current head of the CDU. The daughter of a Lutheran pastor from East Germany, she rose rapidly in the ranks of the CDU following Germany's reunification in 1990. But Merkel and other leaders head Christian Democrat parties that have undergone a lot of change since Germany rose from the ashes after World War II.

The pressures of the revolution in social and cultural attitudes of the 1960s, rising prosperity, and other forces of secularization in European societies put considerable pressure on Christian Democrat parties to retain their vote share in the face of electorates less identified with Christian belief and practice. The most common form of adaptation has been to play down the "confessional" foundations of Christian Democracy—the appeal to observant Christians, and the expectation of a common Christian commitment among supporters—in favor of commitment to only the *political* principles and practices of Christian Democracy. This is possible because some of the principles have become widely accepted beyond their confessional origins. "Subsidiarity," for example, began life as a specifically Roman Catholic term to refer to the irreplaceable contribution families, schools, businesses, and charities make to society, a contribution that government must make legal room for, restraining its own power. Now subsidiarity has grown beyond the rarified atmosphere of Catholic encyclicals to become a broad secular principle. It now refers not only to relations between government and non-governmental institutions, as just described, but also to relations among levels of government. This came about especially during the development of the European Union, with its altered relations among local, national, and newly "supranational" government entities. The latter included the major governing institutions of the Union itself, the European Parliament, Commission, and Court. Other principles of Catholic social teaching, such as human dignity, solidarity, and the common good, have also made the transition from inward-looking principles for thinking about society in a Catholic manner to principles broadly employed to describe standards in European society, principles embraced by many outside the churches altogether. As one scholar remarked of the transition, one could be a Christian Democrat without believing in God.[2]

Konrad Adenauer resigned as Chancellor of West Germany in 1963. In his seventeen-year tenure, he had presided over the writing of Germany's postwar constitution, extended a package of reparations to the Jewish community, forced his opponents to come into loyal opposition as non-Marxist social democrats, and helped build a stronger Europe, both in the form of the fledgling European Community and of a stronger NATO. West Germany had experienced an economic miracle. And in the social capitalism promoted by the CDU, the combination of free enterprise with a social safety net inspired by the Catholic emphasis on human dignity had surely made an important contribution.

For all of his achievements, which reflect Christian Democratic principles, Adenauer was not enamored of certain features usually associated with that perspective. He did not, for example, express much enthusiasm for a multiparty system, regarding it as a source of instability. Instead, he looked to the two-party politics of Britain and the United States for the emphatic verdicts associated with elections in those countries: elections typically gave one party a mandate to govern that it held until the next scheduled elections.[3] The appeal of his CDU was such that, despite the system of proportional representation,[4] which encourages a multiparty system, the party won an overall majority in the lower house of parliament.

2. Van Kersbergen, "The Distinctiveness of Christian Democracy."

3. The observant reader will realize that Adenauer's vote of approval for the decisive Anglo-American democracies pre-dates the rise of polarized politics, in which elections seem to bring more gridlock than decisiveness!

4. Proportional representation (PR) election systems are many but the common element is that political parties receive seats in the legislature in proportion to their share of the popular vote. They achieve this in a range of ways including multi-member districts in which voters cast ballots for political parties and parties' candidates fill seats according to their party's vote share. This is in sharp contrast to the single-member district systems in the UK and US, systems that discourage smaller parties. But under PR a small party does not need to win district by district. If they secure even a modest vote share, that is usually enough to give them some seats. See chapter 8 for a more detailed discussion.

One might say, then, that Adenauer was strong in support of those elements of Catholic teaching on society that fit into his view of a revitalized Germany in a strong West—and that he drew strength from the Catholic perspective in his detestation of Communism. Thus, the principled and the pragmatic were interwoven in ways that defy easy disentangling. Whatever we may make of this particular model of bringing Christian principles to politics and policy, we will find this interweaving to be common to all models claiming Christian inspiration.

In summary, the Adenauer period teaches several lessons. First and foremost, it demonstrates that organized, lay Christian activity can harmonize highly effectively with the democratic process. That activity appears to harmonize most effectively when a response is constructed for the long haul and not in reaction to a single issue. Christian Democrats built organizations to last and they built them for the arena they were working in—politics and government in a representative democracy. In the same way that churches are effective instruments for organizing worship, communicating Christian teachings, and providing for fellowship and service, so political parties are effective means of articulating and defending a political stance and organizing support for that stance.

The German Christian Democrat experience suggests that it may be better to come to Christian political reflection with political experience already in hand, rather than seeking to construct a political orientation out of whole theological cloth, so to speak: one's theological insights will gain traction from one's political experience. Christian political activity never occurs in a vacuum, but necessarily responds to unique sets of circumstances. Integrating prudence with principle is the natural outcome of bringing political experience together with Christian teaching. But it is also worth asking, is the integration evenhanded? Is one of the two values the real driver of the union between them? And what are the consequences that follow?

German social capitalism demonstrates you don't have to argue from socialist presuppositions in order to develop extensive public services in health care and social services. American conservative politicians have achieved lots of success linking any and every welfare state initiative directly to socialism and the totalitarian narrative—successfully because it contrasts so sharply with American liberty and limited government aspirations and handily demonizes political opponents. Given this reality and the highly polarized nature of American politics, the German lesson may fall on deaf ears, but Christians should not be among the deaf.

If Adenauer showed that there were circumstances under which democracy could be shown to be "unthinkable except as a derivative of Christianity,"[5] the time-sensitive character of that demonstration serves as a warning. The contemporary American situation after the Cold War differs sharply from the circumstances the CDU confronted after World War II. With the Soviet threat removed by several decades, the greater challenge lies closer to home—with concepts and values thought to be familiar. Here, "democracy" is now aggressively associated with relativism, expanding individual choice, and equality. It is widely held that religious principles retard democratic development. Undoubtedly the American separation of church and state, and its popular interpretation that religion and politics occupy mutually exclusive jurisdictions with little to say to each other, contributes to this impression. We will take that up in the next chapter.

There is another, related warning in the Christian Democracy story, which pulls in the opposite direction. As Hugh Heclo and Robert Kraynak have separately argued, Christianity has usually served democracy better than democracy has served Christianity. What they mean is that Christianity is vulnerable to being repackaged in the language and norms of democracy. If Christian leaders try too hard to present the faith in the language of egalitarianism and individual freedom, its teachings on sin, repentance, forgiveness, salvation, and Christ's return as King risk being discarded or de-emphasized. Concurrently, the faith shrinks to a set of political positions. And of course if, or when, this occurs, then Christianity will be associated with what it opposes, and perhaps with little else.

Behind these two concerns lie others. Democracy inspires ideas of social leveling, which may challenge the very idea of the kingdom of God. Democracy also proves capable of converting the Christian message of hope—Christ is risen!—into nothing more than a set of political programs loosely related to Christian moral teaching. Christians should certainly look to Christian moral teaching for guidance on policy matters, but support for time-and-situation–specific policies should never convert these into a substitute for hope. Politics is not about ultimate questions! It is about working with limited resources toward partial solutions of problems that change and recur and never yield perfection. Christian Democracy also risks blurring the distinctions between church and state. We will return to all these concerns in later chapters. For the moment, let me simply

---

5. Cary, *The Path to Christian Democracy*, 276.

ask the question that I posed in the first chapter, but direct it to post-World War II Christian Democracy in Germany:

Is *this* Christian politics?

Let me first make the positive case. Obviously, Christian Democracy constitutes *a version* of something that could be called "Christian politics." It should get Christians' attention for just that reason, I think. Its distinctive features commend it to us—a strong commitment to reconciliation, across class lines especially, but by extension to other divides such as those shaped by gender, race, or religion itself; a commitment to social capitalism; and a commitment to the integrity of the family as a vital, irreplaceable social agency. Reconciliatory policies between labor and management proved economically fruitful and undoubtedly made a positive contribution to the German "economic miracle." Social capitalism combined free market principles with a sizeable social safety net. Under Christian Democracy, family policy was generous and protective. Universal health care and social insurance policies were supported, although in the German case neither originated with Christian Democracy. All of this, the principles, the policies, and the politics, deserves careful examination.

To associate Christian Democracy with certain policies is not the same thing as saying that Christian commitment to politics is only authentic *if* it embraces those particular policies at all times and in all circumstances. One may make such a claim as far as *principles* are concerned, but policies are the strategic responses to various sets of circumstances, in a particular time and place. They are bounded by these circumstances to a degree, and are not constructed in the abstract. The important question to ask is how well the policies linked to particular circumstances reflect the unchanging principles.

Earlier Catholic initiatives in Bismarck's Germany (1871–1890) help explain the point. When Adenauer helped found the CDU he was determined to distance it from the older Catholic Center Party—with which he had been much involved earlier in his political career. The Center Party was formed in response to the anti-Catholic policies of Chancellor Bismarck. It was a "sectarian" party, a party *for Catholics*. The party gave Catholics an organization in the parliament and a way of defending their practices and their integrity against laws that undermined them. This was particularly important in connection to education policy, which restricted the scope of Catholic schools.

Adenauer could understand the importance of defending a Catholic perspective but he had no intention of constructing a "fortress" party for Catholics alone in 1945. In the aftermath of the war, which had left his country under Allied, and therefore partly Soviet communist, occupation, Adenauer wanted the CDU to represent the entire Judeo-Christian civilization of the West. This could not be accomplished if the CDU represented just one group of Germans. The CDU could retain a clear perspective (or world view) but should not be a "confessing" party in the narrower sense of one whose supporters were more or less required to be churchgoing, observant Catholics. As Noel Cary puts it, Adenauer positioned the CDU in the political system to make it appear that "democracy in Germany was not possible except as a derivative of Christianity . . . ."[6]

So, as we can see, Christian politics in Germany took on distinctly different forms in the nineteenth and twentieth centuries. Each form represented a calculated response to a distinct set of circumstances. Let me suggest that Christian political reflection, and action, will *always* have at its center the relationship between universal principles and unique circumstances. It will always be "located" between this world and the next.

Principles command loyalty, while unique circumstances will call for strategic responses. Deciding how to act in response to circumstances always involves some balancing of the two. After the fact, when the party organization has been founded or the march organized or the lobbying undertaken, people will ask all sorts of questions: was the action sufficiently loyal to Christian principles? Was it the appropriate response or would another have been more effective? What were the unintended consequences?

By the 1990s, Europe was profoundly transformed. The transformation included rapid secularization and declining church attendance. In some European countries, France for example, a Christian Democratic party was formed that later collapsed. In other countries, it had barely gotten off the ground. The old enemy, Soviet communism, fell politically and spiritually, and a remarkable transition to democracy emerged in all the old Warsaw Pact countries. New Christian Democratic parties emerged in several of these countries.

In the newly united German federal republic, the political effects of secularization were somewhat delayed by the merging of the Christian Democratic parties from the former East and West Germanys. The former renewed, for a while, the confessional emphasis of Christian Democracy as a party influenced by active Christian belief and practice.

However, the forces of secularization were only checked, not reversed. Across western Europe, Christian Democrat parties adapted in important

6. Ibid.

ways. They stressed their political values over those values' Christian origins. In the words of former Dutch prime minister Ruud Lubbers, they chose to stress the trans-Christian appeal of those values.[7]

Christian Democrat values certainly retained, and still retain, considerable appeal. When your author visited the Dutch Christian Democratic party's (CDA) think tank in 2001, the topic for discussion that day was the rise toward leadership status of some of its Muslim members. Why the interest in Christian Democracy from followers of Islam? The answer lay largely in education policy. For roughly a century, Dutch education policy had explicitly made room for basic beliefs in the way that schools are run. Government funds schools but parents as governors have considerable influence in how schools are run. Thus a system of secular, Catholic, and Calvinist schools emerged. Such a pluralist system of schooling, subsidized by government, would prove attractive to religious minorities of many kinds, not to Christians alone.

When you go to the websites of today's Christian Democrat parties, the accommodation to secularized Europe appears complete. Expressly religious influence is acknowledged but usually confined to brief sections on the party's history. But even if any kind of confessional influence is downplayed, one has only to look at policy statements to see their dependence on such (usually Roman Catholic) principles as subsidiarity, solidarity, and the common good.

But we should press the question. Is this rebalancing of principles and circumstances a retreat to a weaker version of Christian politics? Is the most authentic version what I have called a "confessional" model in which the party leaders and members are expected to be observant believers?

Of course, this distinction and the questions I have posed merely pose other questions. Should we treat either model as having a robust claim to Christian faithfulness in the first place? Both models assume that organized political activity is appropriate for believers. Shouldn't that question be explored first?

Students from evangelical backgrounds have sometimes asked me if Christian political activity should be tied closely to evangelism. They take the position that the highest priority for Christians should be Jesus's Great Commission at the end of Matthew's gospel, to make disciples of all nations. So, they ask, shouldn't that be the goal of political engagement? And if it should be the goal, what form would *a politics of evangelism* take? Does

7. Sherratt, "Christian Democracy in America?"

it call for Christians to organize political parties or should a quite different approach be taken? What sorts of organizations would it call for?

Another line of questions casts doubt on the whole idea of a "distinctly Christian," or biblical, approach to politics. The usual objection is that it will send all the wrong messages—that Christians are exclusive, or think they are morally superior, "holier than thou." To many critics, that impression far outweighs any good the party might do. Others pose a closely related objection. To create a party based on biblical values or Christian ideals—however the commitment is expressed—is false advertising because Christian traditions are many and varied and such a party would only attract some Christians. Look at all the groups, sects, and denominations in the United States. How could you ever unite Baptists and Catholics and Mennonites in the same political movement—or, for that matter, how would you get all Catholics or all Baptists to subscribe to the same political orientation? So, what business would such a party have claiming the Christian label for itself?

Each of these questions deserves a hearing and I hope to give them one as we proceed. What I would invite readers to do first, however, is to acquire as much knowledge as they can about actual historical or contemporary Christian political initiatives. We can engage questions like these most effectively if we ask them against the background of acquaintance with Christian political activity. If we know something about the Christian Right—and the Christian Left—in the United States, and if we know that German, Dutch, French, and Italian Catholics, with some Protestants, in more or less the same time period, went beyond lobbying on this or that policy issue and formed political parties, something the vast majority of American Christians have avoided altogether, we will be that much better equipped to ask such important questions.

The richer our grasp of what Christians have done, the better placed we will be to wrestle with the theology and political theory that these questions raise. Yes, it really does matter for politics whether Christians are called to evangelize in all areas of life as their top priority. It really does matter that we understand the tasks of politics—what government and politics are *for*.

German circumstances encouraged Konrad Adenauer and his colleagues to frame a distinctive strategic response that has given us, several decades further on, a rich and complex case study to explore as we search for Christian perspective on politics and government. The first chapter explored how American evangelical Christians have responded to political and social challenges in this country. Comparing these two sets of initiatives, we can discern that each was in its own way a response to local circumstances. But that may in turn undermine the idea that there is, or even should be, a single model of Christian politics.

Conclusion

Christian Democracy and the Religious Right have each left a large footprint on the political landscape of the democratic West since the middle of the last century. I suggest that no fresh initiative that aspires to a politics informed by Christian understanding can afford to ignore them. For contemporary Christians in the United States, these are the models to begin with, not because they are attractive in themselves or because they represent perfection but because together these models raise almost all the pertinent questions for Christian political engagement.

The two models differ considerably, as we have seen. Christian Democracy got off the ground by launching a political party. The Religious Right experimented with single-issue interest groups before turning to "colonization" efforts in state Republican parties.[8] From the beginning, the CDU possessed a full-fledged philosophy of government. No such philosophy emerged in the Religious Right, which embraced a blend of Christian moralism, patriotism, and, ironically but logically, Enlightenment views of individual liberty.

Writing around the turn of the present century, Michael Fogarty, a leading scholar of Christian Democracy, examined the two models and reached the surprising conclusion that they had more in common than meets the eye. He referred to Christian Democracy (with an uppercase *D*) to denote the high level of political development of the European model and Christian democracy (with a lowercase *d*) to describe the American model with its inclination toward interest group activity and its ongoing search for identity as it makes an uneasy home in the politics of the GOP. He treated the differences between them as differences in organization and strategy but not necessarily in goals. And he went further. An active Christian Democrat himself, Fogarty suggested that the two models merge, interact, and learn from each other.[9]

---

8. There was, of course, no Religious Right as such until these efforts had matured to some degree and the mix of groups and strategies had begun to approximate a movement. The label followed recognition that some kind of movement existed.

9. See Fogarty, *Motorways Merge*.

The burden of Fogarty's argument is equal parts pragmatism and confessional faithfulness. The rise of secularization, at a different pace in Europe and the United States, brings a common opponent into cultural and political discourse, and the effect everywhere has been to push old religious foes toward each other, if not into each other's arms. So, for example, under the leadership of such Catholic and evangelical luminaries as Richard John Neuhaus and Charles Colson in the United States, religious leaders issued in 1994 a confession for past sins and a commitment to seek the common Christian mission together. This initiative reflected the similar rapprochement between Roman Catholic and Reformed Protestant parties in the Netherlands and Belgium, which merged into Christian Democrat parties in the postwar period. At its founding, the CDU reached beyond denominational politics to a common Christian world view and toward a sensibility that was neither Protestant nor Catholic.

By the end of the twentieth century, Christian Democracy had adapted to a secularized European electorate. For the most part, it had set aside pretensions to confessional politics, begging the question how long its Christian values would remain in place. As noted in the first chapter, the Religious Right appeared to have made little change to core commitments and principles, at the price of high levels of hostility and undiminished polarization between the two major political parties.

Christian politics could take different forms from these two models. I suspect, however, that such models would either not exist on the same scale or would put more distance between faith and politics, or would play down an organized presence in the political arena. Any of these may appear to readers more attractive options. However, we are unlikely to fashion alternatives without careful study of these two large models.

What I want to do next is to try to do just that, to rethink the project of Christian political engagement from the theological ground up as it were. But we must leave open the possibility that the rethinking will point us in some familiar directions and that we may end up deciding not to reinvent the wheel after all.

Chapter 3 _____

Christ is Risen!

Christ is King

CHRIST IS RISEN! THE Lord is risen indeed! This is the Easter greeting Christians have exchanged from the earliest days of the church. "Very early on the morning of the third day," the Gospel writers tell us, some of the women among Jesus' disciples went to the tomb in which his body had been placed in order to anoint the body with spices. On arrival, they found the tomb empty. Jesus then appeared to the disciples on several occasions, appearances that convinced those disciples that the person who appeared and with whom they spoke was Jesus. On the one hand, the dead do not come back from death. On the other, he spoke with them; he ate with them. At least one of the disciples, "Doubting" Thomas, insisted that before he could believe he place his fingers in the holes made by the nails and spears of the Roman soldiers who conducted the crucifixion. On more than one occasion Jesus' appearance and his departure was sudden and not normal, in that he did not seem to enter the room but simply to appear. On other occasions, he met the disciples, on the shore of Lake Galilee and on the road to Emmaus for example, and was not recognized until some characteristic action revealed his identity. Some while after these appearances, Jesus "ascended." Here again, the writers report a phenomenon outside their readers' comprehension of how the physical universe functions and invite those readers to believe that it occurred.

When a Christian writes of Jesus' resurrection and ascension, then, the reader knows that the foundation for what (s)he writes are these eyewitness accounts, together with Jesus' repeated, and repeatedly ignored, prophecies that he would be crucified, rise again after three days, and ascend to God the Father (Mark 8:31).

Jesus' resurrection sets the context for everything else in Christianity. It makes good on his teaching, as the disciples themselves eventually realized. Jesus taught that those who denied themselves for the sake of the good news would receive eternal life in the age to come. He had demonstrated that he believed his own words by willingly surrendering his own life, and in his resurrection and ascension. The New Testament writers, especially the author of the Letter to the Hebrews, explain how Jesus' death, resurrection, and ascension make sense of the entire trajectory of Hebrew Scripture, including the eyewitness accounts of Jesus' contemporaries, as telling the story of creation, fall, redemption, and judgment.

Jesus' moral teaching, epitomized in the Sermon on the Mount, is not theologically separable from the good news of his resurrection. "Christ is risen!" is an even more demanding and challenging claim than the command to "Love your enemies!" The moral teaching is demanding, of course! But it challenges our will, not our credulity. The resurrection may only be received by faith. It asks us to believe that something happened that we couldn't conceive of having happened. Neither a layman's nor a scientist's understanding of the physical universe explains this to us. Instead, explanations from either of those sources push in the opposite direction to the account recorded in the Gospels. People do not rise from the dead. To assert that they do is to fly in the face of ordinary experience and scientific principles.

Writing in Britain's *Daily Telegraph* in 2013, journalist and biographer A. N. Wilson pinpointed Christian beliefs of this kind as exactly the thing that his contemporaries cannot accept, and then made the all-too-predictable jump to the moral preoccupations on the minds of postmoderns. "Most people simply cannot subscribe to the traditional creeds," he wrote. "No number of Alpha courses can make people believe that God took human form of a Virgin, or rose from the dead. They simply can't swallow it. They see no reason, therefore, to listen to a Church that propounds these stories and then presumes to tell them how to behave in the bedroom."[1]

Whatever we make of the claim that Christ is risen, the accounts given by Matthew, Mark, Luke, and John connect the resurrection and the moral teaching closely. The resurrection places the moral teaching firmly in a supernatural context, as its inseparable corollary. Christ is risen, *so,* love your enemies. In other words, the moral teaching is inseparable from the biblical narrative of creation, fall, redemption, and judgment. It takes its

---

1. Wilson, "Lord Carey's Vision for the Church Might Kill It Off."

bearings, so to speak, from that narrative and from the supernatural hope of a reconciliation with God and the renewal of creation with which it ends.

I should pause here to make a point of clarification in response to this last observation. "Supernatural" has many an unhelpful connotation, from the ghostly to the weird and everything in between! But the New Testament writers do not contrast the physical universe with a nonphysical dimension, nor do they suggest that Jesus was raised from the dead to take up residence in such a dimension. No, Jesus was raised to bring his kingship to the good world that God made, to free it from the workings of evil, and to raise it to an even *more* substantial "reality" than the merely physical.

C. S. Lewis's *The Great Divorce,* in which a party of residents of hell are granted a holiday in heaven, provides a powerful literary image of this more substantial reality. For the vacationers from hell, preoccupied as they are with their own sense of justice and the injustices inflicted on them, heaven is unappealing. It's too real. They walk on its lawns and the blades of grass lacerate the soles of their feet. Christ's coming kingdom, the New Testament insists, ushers in real justice and real joy, and its citizens will be renewed in their faculties, to "mount up, with wings like eagles, they will run and not be weary, they shall walk and not faint" (Isa 40:31 RSV).

To receive this good news takes faith. We should recall here T. S. Eliot's observation that humans "cannot bear very much reality."[2] Jesus' disciples step out in faith in memorable ways. At Jesus' invitation, Peter climbs out of his boat and begins walking to Jesus across the surface of the stormy lake. Sent out by Jesus on a healing mission, some seventy disciples come back babbling with astonishment at the power they have exercised. "Even the demons submit to us in your name!" (Luke 10:17 NIV). The willingness to exercise faith is often stronger outside the circle of Jesus' disciples than inside it. A centurion, an officer in the occupying Roman army no less, asks the Jewish rabbi to heal his servant. But he hesitates to ask Jesus to come into his house for the purpose. "Lord, I do not deserve to have you come under my roof. But just say the word, and my servant will be healed" (Matt 8:8 NIV). Jesus commends the faith of this pagan official above any he has found in Israel before assuring him that his servant has been healed.

As Peter and the other disciples take first one step and then another in, and into, their faith in Jesus, powerful tensions emerge. Recall Peter's horrified reaction when Jesus tells the disciplines he is going to be betrayed and killed. Peter rejects the possibility outright. This earns him the strictest

2. Eliot, *Four Quartets,* 14.

of rebukes from Jesus: "Get behind me, Satan." But this is no mere rebuke. It is a genuine correction. The divine power in which Peter has trusted correlates to suffering, service, and weakness, but repels comfort, status, and coercion. The Peter of the Gospels cannot grasp this. Following the resurrection, however, the Peter of Acts and the epistles is a man converted.

We should not be surprised, then, that it should be Peter who articulates a believer's faith commitment most poignantly. Faced with these hard teachings, many disciples had apparently stopped following Jesus, so John's Gospel records. Jesus asks the twelve whether they, too, will leave. Peter replies, "Lord, to whom can we go? You have the words of eternal life" (John 6:68 NIV). For the believer, there *is* nowhere else to go. Peter has chosen to live by faith in Jesus. All his eggs are in that basket.

Peter's choice carries over into every area of life. So does ours. Take an ordinary example of Christian action. When Christians volunteer for acts of service and support, their decision to do so has its origins in belief in the resurrection. As N. T. Wright puts it, "They aren't volunteering because the government has told them we can't afford to pay for such work any more. They do it because of Jesus."[3] Wright goes on:

> When God wants to change the world, he doesn't send in the tanks (as many, including many critics, think he should). He sends in the meek; and by the time the world realizes what's going on, the meek have set up clinics and schools, taught people to read and to sing, and given them a hope, meaning and purpose which secular modernism (which gave us, after all, Passchendaele and Auschwitz as well as modern medicine and space travel) has failed to provide.

In response to Wright's book, *Surprised by Hope*, Mari Williams wrote that the message of Christian hope had deepened several of her commitments to service, commitments that were in many respects discouraging with mixed results. She described how she worked for a Christian service agency focused on justice in global trade. Successes were few, defeats many. Was it all a waste of time, she asks?

> Before, I'd have said no, it's still right to challenge injustice—whatever the outcome.
>
> Now, I'd still say that, but there's more. According to Wright, actions such as working for justice for the poor, done in love and

---

3. Wright, "Keep the Faith." New Testament scholar N. T. Wright is the former Bishop of Durham (UK).

obedience to Scripture, in the power of the spirit, will be *completed and fulfilled* in the new Kingdom. They are not wasted. Now THAT is hope![4]

It follows, I think, that to ask what an authentic Christian perspective on any subject should look like, government and politics included, requires us to accept the resurrection as the necessary condition behind Christian action. It alone gives Christians hope. It alone sets earthly suffering in its eternal[5] context. The supernatural foundations of Christianity make up the real setting in which Christians operate, the lodestar from which they take their bearings. Authentic Christianity may involve much more than this foundation, but it cannot be based on anything less.

To all sorts of people, of course, whether they are A. N. Wilson's English postmodernists or their American equivalents, perhaps there's just too much to swallow here. Virgin birth, resurrection, healings, water into wine, all somehow adding up to love and offered as our hope, are simply incredible, so the step of faith to embrace them cannot be taken. And certainly, if Jesus cannot heal, and did not rise from death after his crucifixion, then we may doubt his ability to forgive or his claim to be God and King.

The Christian Paradox: Power Made Perfect in Weakness

Christians affirming this most central declaration of the Christian confession of faith also affirm several principles relevant for politics and the ways of contemporary culture: They are embracing a framework for political understanding.

God is sovereign, not governments or powerful business people, or revolutionary movements or media, and yet God chooses to exercise

4. Williams, "Surprised by Tom Wright."

5. One could write "heavenly" as a synonym for "eternal" or make some reference to "life everlasting" in the "forever and ever, amen" sense. But "eternal," meaning outside of time, conveys something a bit tighter than any of these. Heaven has too many misleading connotations and each of the other terms is time-bound. Eternal, by contrast, allows for God to be the author of time. It allows Jesus to tell his disciples, "Before Abraham was, I am" (John 8:58 NIV). It allows the resurrected Jesus to have appeared to his disciples and not be recognized, until some action, such as breaking bread (Luke 24:30) enabled them to realize that it was he. In Jesus's post-resurrection appearances he appears suddenly (even in locked rooms), reassures his disciples that he is not a ghost, eats and drinks, and yet is reluctant to allow them to touch him (John 20:17). The final apocalyptic vision of a new (renewed) heavens and earth in the book of Revelation sums up the hope in Jesus that inspires Christians and is inseparable from Christian moral teaching.

his power in a curious and paradoxical way: the central event of the New Testament features a stunning defeat by the worldly powers, followed by a mysterious resolution—the crucifixion and resurrection of Jesus.

The Old Testament prefigures Jesus' crucifixion and resurrection in many instances, some of which are accompanied by commentary that lends insight into the workings of divine power. Take the story of Joseph. The apple of his father's eye, the youngest brother of nine, Joseph earns his siblings' deep resentment. They plan to kill him, and are only persuaded by an unexpected turn of events to sell him into slavery instead. Years later, famine in their homeland drives those same brothers to Egypt, where unknown to them Joseph has become an influential administrator. He gives them sacks of grain to offset the effects of the famine. Of their earlier actions, Joseph remarks, "You intended to harm me, but God intended it for good" (Gen 50:20 NLT). God, Christians believe, is sovereign over all circumstances.

God's sovereignty has always proved perplexing, and its mysterious, contradictory character rises to the most extraordinary of crescendos when the sovereign dies on the cross at the hands of the occupying Roman authorities abetted by compliant Jewish leaders and a fickle populace.

How God works in the world is not to be equated with force or physical strength, or with calculated use of resources to gain advantage. Instead God shows power through service, suffering, sacrifice, humility, hospitality, and shalom. Power is made perfect in weakness. Jesus' obedient sacrifice, his execution by the Roman authorities by crucifixion, forms the highest expression of divine weakness-as-power. These qualities of service, suffering, sacrifice, and the rest, are what I understand to be at least some of the biblical correlates of "weakness." To embrace them, then, means more than acting in a "nice" way. It means to tap into—or better, to cooperate with—the power of God at work in the world. If we are to obey God, this is the way to do so. This is the way to wield true power.

The Scriptures do not confine the principle that power is made perfect in weakness to Jesus' birth, death, and resurrection, although we may confidently view these events as epitomizing the principle and pointing us to its centrality in the life of the world. Consider Jesus' well-known sayings and parables on the subject of sowing, cultivating, reaping, and harvest. There's the parable of the Sower, of course, from Matthew 13. A farmer goes to his field to start a crop. He walks up and down, broadcasting the seeds. Some of them fall on the prepared soil but birds eat it. More fall where the soil is thin, so they does not grow very well. Still more germinate but compete unsuccessfully with weeds for the soil's nutrients. Some fall on the abutting path and are lost. And some fall on good soil and providesthe farmer the crop he hoped for from all of it.

Notice that the seed, the kingdom of God, is sown and is growing *in the world*. The created order of which God is the sovereign does not lie somewhere else, and certainly not somewhere disembodied and merely spiritual. No, the earth lies within the jurisdiction of the kingdom of God. When the seed is planted in the ground it *will* grow, but it can either be choked by weeds, starved of nutrients, or properly cultivated.

"Truly, truly, I say to you, unless a grain of wheat falls into the earth and dies, it remains alone; but if it dies, it bears much fruit" (John 12:24 ESV). In making that declaration, Jesus was speaking of his own coming execution but in the verses that follow he urged his disciples to embrace the same principle: "Anyone who loves their life will lose it, while anyone who hates their life in this world will keep it for eternal life. Whoever serves me must follow me; and where I am, my servant also will be. My Father will honor the one who serves me" (John 12:25–26 NIV).

The power made perfect in weakness is linked explicitly to each person's attitude toward life. Jesus upholds the hope of eternal life and warns us not to try to hold on to our lives but invites us instead to be willing to lose them. Always the promised outcome is the same: growth, fruitfulness, and fullness. This is, of course, the central Christian paradox, illustrated over and over again in parables and metaphors in Jesus' teaching. The way to pursue the full, rich, certain promise of fullness of life is to set fullness of life aside. Instead, the route to be followed seems altogether contradictory, downright unpromising. Deny yourself, "take up your cross," and follow Jesus. Mark records Jesus' teaching as follows:

> Peter began to say to Him, "Behold, we have left everything and followed you." Jesus said, "Truly I say to you, there is no one who has left house or brothers or sisters or mother or father or children or farms, for my sake and for the gospel's sake, but that he will receive a hundred times as much now in the present age, houses and brothers and sisters and mothers and children and farms, along with persecutions; and in the age to come, eternal life . . . " (Mark 10:28-30 NASB).

Of course, as any believer can tell you, just because we can say, "Oh yes, this is the central Christian paradox" doesn't make understanding or resolving that paradox any easier. Self-denial, loss, persecution . . . and fruitfulness—please don't think it's all in a day's work for believers!

Faith is a necessity if we are to claim the truths declared here and to act on them! If you are reading this from outside the Christian faith, please don't think that Christians easily and fully embrace these teachings, either. The stakes seem very high to believers also. Taking up one's cross; losing one's life in order to gain it; seeking God's kingdom above everything else; these and related sayings have an all-or-nothing quality to them that repels even as it attracts.

One of the reasons believers struggle with these truths is that in the developed world, core features of the environment have altered drastically since biblical times. Writing in 2002, Philip Jenkins reminded readers that the vast majority of the world's Christians live in the developing world and can be characterized as poor, powerless, and supernaturalist.[6] By contrast, Christians in the developed world know relatively little poverty, and enjoy political and legal power. As a result, with significant earthly needs accounted for, could it be that our supernaturalist muscles need much more exercise than they usually get to compensate for the transformation of our material and political circumstances? Writing in 2015, one can only contrast these circumstances with those of the Christian communities in the strife-torn Middle East, or sub-Saharan Africa, especially along the fault lines between historically Christian and Muslim areas. Here the New Testament realities are all too fresh and real. Without question, the body of Christ could profit from theological reflection undertaken under such desperate conditions.

The New Testament writers were as aware of the demands of faith as any contemporary Christian. The writer of the Letter to the Hebrews reminds the reader of the "great cloud of witnesses" made up of the faithful through the ages who lived out lives of faith without ever seeing the promises redeemed in their lifetimes. As noted earlier, the Gospel writers record Jesus commending the faith of those outside the faith—a Roman centurion, a Samaritan woman—for recognizing his authority and trusting him. Certainly even genuinely faithful members of the church have no corner on living faithfully. We certainly don't do it automatically. Every Christian finds him- or herself in the position of the father seeking healing for his son, recorded in Mark's gospel. He searches out Jesus with a mixture of desperation and doubt, wanting his son healed, yet skeptical that such

---

6. Jenkins, *The Next Christendom.*

a thing can happen. Jesus tells him, "All things are possible for one who believes." In anguished response, the man cries, "Lord, I believe. Help my unbelief" (Mark 9:24 ESV). That's all of us, isn't it?

Fellowship is necessary, too, of course. What the New Testament can do for each individual believer, it can magnify for the body of believers, the church. Believers strengthen their faith by practicing it. I mean "practice" in both senses in which we use the word. We practice the piano to get better at it. And a doctor practices medicine as her professional vocation. We practice the faith by worshipping with other believers, giving thanks to God, receiving instruction in the faith, praying for ours and others' needs, and in trying to meet the physical and spiritual needs we find around us in our churches and surrounding communities—both to get better at it (to develop the habit, if you like) and to follow our calling.

Le Chambon

One of the more astonishing contemporary accounts of the power made perfect comes from France during the Second World War. It is a story that has been told many times over so many reading this will already know of it. Recently, it played a role in author Malcolm Gladwell's return to faith. I include it here for the way it testifies to a faith-filled, obedient Christianity.

When France fell to the German armies in 1940, a large section of the country did not come under direct German supervision. Instead, the German authorities permitted the organization of a puppet French administration, the so-called Vichy government—named for the spa town in which it was convened. The Vichy government's jurisdiction extended officially to the whole of the country except for eastern regions annexed to Germany, but in practice was subservient to the military occupying forces in northern and western France and governed on its own only in the southern region of the country, the Zone Libre.

Le Chambon-sur-Lignon, a small hill town not far from Lyons, lay in this so-called free zone. When the Vichy government began to deport Jews to concentration camps in 1942, Le Chambon's Protestant pastor, André Trocmé, urged his congregation to do what they could to give shelter to Jews and other refugees whose lives were threatened by Nazi policies. Until the end of the war, somewhere between three and five thousand people were helped by the community who housed many and helped others escape into Switzerland. Trocmé embraced Jews as the people of the Old Testament but chiefly impressed on his congregation the Christian obligation simply to shelter those in need. No doubt their own history as descendants of France's persecuted Huguenots gave the people of Le Chambon a sense of solidarity with another persecuted minority, too.

Pastor Trocmé did not hide his obligation to shelter the persecuted from the Vichy authorities, including on one occasion a minister in the Vichy government. It is this combination of simple obedience—obeying the command to help one's neighbor—with open witness to the source of that command, Jesus Christ, to say nothing of the ever-present risks he was willing to take, that forms such a powerful testimony.

The story of Le Chambon and "how goodness happened there"[7] deserves a much fuller telling than this brief summary. I cite it here because it gathers together the twin truths that form the title to this chapter and acts as a bridge from the one to the other. Christ is risen. Christ is king. On the basis of these elemental truths of the Christian faith, an entire community defied a government backed by law and the military might of an occupying power to exercise true power. I write "elemental" to emphasize the sheer simplicity of the Trocmé's exercise of faith and its fruitful outcome in the face of evil. This could be called childlike faith, recalling Jesus' warning, "Truly I tell you, unless you change and become like little children, you will never enter the kingdom of heaven" (Matt 18:3 NIV).

Christ is King

In *How God Became King,* N. T. Wright organizes his argument by means of a resonant metaphor. His subject matter is the story that the Gospels tell. The writings of Matthew, Mark, Luke, and John contain four interwoven themes. Think of the gospel as a quadraphonic masterpiece and of these themes, Wright suggests, as four "speakers." Together, they carry the entire narrative. Separately, they make unique contributions to the richness of the whole. Today, however, Christians are denied much of that polyphonic wealth. It is as if one or two of the speakers have been turned up, drowning out the others and distorting and truncating the good news itself.

Common to all four themes is the paradox of kingdom and cross, or as I have described it, the paradox of the power made perfect in weakness. As Wright explains, Jesus' suffering does not precede his kingdom but is in fact the means by which he inaugurates it. He exercises power within the

---

7. The full story is told by Hallie, *Lest Innocent Blood be Shed.*

terms of his suffering. The cross is kingdom work, the kingdom "at work," one could say.

The four themes are as follows: First, Jesus is the climax of the story of Israel, of God's chosen people. Second, Jesus, the Good Shepherd, will save his people. Third, by means of his death on the cross, Jesus inaugurates a transformed Israel, a renewed people of God and in this way the kingdom breaks in on the world and its cultures. And finally, the kingdom and cross confront Caesar's world at the deepest level. God deals with Adam's sin and the problem of evil.

In our Christian churches, and even to some extent in the church's ancient creeds, the second and third themes receive most amplification, Wright argues. Jesus died for my sins and in the church we have the experience of renewed human fellowship. But even here, there is distortion. The message of salvation is amplified chiefly as an individual matter. True though it is that Jesus died for my sins, this dimension of the good news should not drown out the message of salvation for God's people as a people. As for suffering and persecution, these themes are given very little consideration as this-worldly accompaniments to the Christian way. In reality, Wright insists, Christians are, and should think of themselves as, "suffering kingdom bringers."[8] To put it less elegantly than he does, this is how the power of God in the world *works*.

If the second and third themes come across somewhat distorted, we have to strain our ears even to catch the presence of the first and fourth themes. And yet it should be hard, for example, to understand the fury of the Jewish authorities condemning Jesus before Pilate without an understanding of the nature of his offense in their eyes. To the chief priests, Jesus is a heretic and a blasphemer, claiming powers that belong to God alone—especially the power to forgive sins. But this claim holds up, the writers of the Gospels insist, for in Jesus' life, death, and resurrection we reach the climax of the story of Israel.

As for the fourth theme, Jesus' confrontation with the powers and principalities, or their representatives in pagan culture and political authority, barely registers in most Christian teaching and worship. There are many plausible explanations, but let me concentrate on just two with the American context in mind. First, however strained the relationship between church and state, or religion and politics, is becoming, elements of the settlement that Hugh Heclo hailed as the Great Denouement remain in

---

8. Wright, *How God Became King*, 201–2.

place. You may recall this from chapter 1. Strife between Democrats and Republicans has plenty of faith-based input but religious liberty remains an American reality. Perhaps it is for this reason that it is hard to appreciate just how central to the New Testament is the confrontation between God and the powers.

To come at this part of Wright's argument from a different angle, in most evangelical churches, the message of salvation is given immediate, direct, relevant, and urgent attention. So, too, in a different sense, making the church attractive to its members and would-be members is given immediate, direct, relevant, and urgent attention. Attractive worship, compelling programs of service, mission and outreach, excellent Sunday school offerings, and the like all testify to the presumed "core" of the Christian message—Jesus died for your sins. Accept his forgiveness and his gift of new life. The declaration that "Christ is King" is not so much denied as starved for attention, given the attention these priorities attract.

Politics from the Perspective of Christ, the Risen King

The good news that Christ is the risen King has profound implications for politics. If Wright is right, that teaching is barely audible in our churches, so these implications go similarly unheard. Thankfully, we can turn to a well-developed tradition of Christian thinking to make up the deficit.

Abraham Kuyper (1837–1920) epitomizes the substance and perhaps also the stereotype of the term "Victorian." Pastor; politician; philosopher; journalist; founder of newspapers, a university, and a political party; writer of devotionals; and prime minister of the Netherlands, he exemplifies the larger-than-life world of the late nineteenth century, populated as it was by explorers, imperialists, novelists, composers, and romantics. It was an age in which European empires appeared to enjoy a solid hold on their possessions. It would be the twentieth century before they turned on one another and destroyed themselves in the process. The Victorian era seemed set to last forever, despite the changes surging beneath the surface. Not a hundred years separated it from the French Revolution, and the ideas disseminated by that revolution were already making themselves felt as the traditional societies of Europe were obliged to accommodate an upsurge of democratic ideas. Industrial revolution brought undreamt of prosperity, unimagined squalor, and a revolutionary political philosophy in Marxism that would upend politics altogether in the century to come.

Kuyper was a careful student of all these developments, especially the rise of democracy, and as a Calvinist Christian his political interests posed fundamental questions he took pains to answer. Chief among them was how the sovereignty of governments could be squared with the sovereignty of God. Democracy declared that the people were the source of political sovereignty. But only God was truly sovereign.

Kuyper did not occupy an ivory tower. As pastor, journalist, and political leader this question confronted him as the most practical of questions. The French Revolution had marched under the slogan "Neither God nor Master" and in its hostility to both monarchy and church and its declaration of the rights of man, Kuyper recognized a philosophical revolution that his Christian conscience could not accept. Government, even in a democratic let alone a revolutionary incarnation, was not ordained by the people, but by God.

Governments could only enjoy a limited scope of authority, Kuyper thought, for two reasons. On the one hand, he thought it was self-evident that human beings could not claim universal competence, let alone a matching authority and power. On the other, on the same principle by which God ordains human *governments*, God also conveys sovereignty to other *nongovernmental* social bodies. The human task of bearing God's image to the creation does not consist of a single task, let alone a task that belongs only to government, but is made up of many responsibilities. The relationship of master to steward encapsulates the human responsibility to care for and nurture God's creation. Families undertake tasks of stewardship. So do farmers. So do small businesses, government regulatory agencies, and charities. And if all these agencies make unique contributions to stewardship of creation, then all of them, including governments, must make room for the others. It isn't just governments that can be violators of sphere sovereignty. In his day, Kuyper thought that the Catholic Church was guilty of violations. In the twentieth century, popes condemned the totalitarian governments for flagrant violations. In our own day, we may wonder about the role played by global corporations in the economic life of nations and regions.

Kuyper understood sovereignty as "authority that possesses the right and duty, and wields the power to break and punish all resistance to its will." His conscience, and he thought everyone's conscience, showed that this power could only be God's. It could not "reside in any creature, but must coincide with the majesty of God."[9]

9. Kuyper, *Sphere Sovereignty*, 3.

Human authority had also to be limited within each domain or sphere, Kuyper thought, on account of sin. To put it another way, we encounter families, businesses, and governments in profoundly broken condition. The culprits are distressingly familiar, among them greed, abuse, neglect, and lust. Original sin thwarts what Kuyper took to be the ideal—a global government under God, essentially—a view he held on the basis that all humans are of "one blood." Nation-states are the next best thing. They do not really suit our human nature, he thought. All the same, even in this form, the state exists to check the effects of sin.

In his Calvinist theological frame of reference, Kuyper's view of political authority was significantly influenced by the distinction between common and particular grace. By common grace, he meant the grace of God toward the entire creation. God sends the rain to fall on the just and the unjust alike (Matt 5:45), to use a common example. Creation (or nature, for Kuyper saw these as interchangeable) always benefited in this way from God's grace, despite the effects of sin. Particular grace, that is, the saving grace of God, offered the hope of a creation recovered and renewed.

Through this lens, we may understand why Kuyper treated earthly political authority cautiously. There is a profound realism here, with no hint of utopian optimism for human political systems. Sphere sovereignty, this principle by which human agencies take up the multiple tasks of stewardship, is not a blueprint for a perfect society, let alone a perfect government. It aims instead at earthly justice, to be achieved to the extent fallible human beings reflect God's creation ordinances in a fallen world. The state is an agent of common grace. Its task is to sustain creation, not to redeem it. But the justice it attempts to bring, by limiting its own scope and helping other human agencies to flourish as best they can, is at the same time in cooperation with the God who *does* save, and who *will* redeem the entire created order.

Much of the work of the state is, then, quite modest—and focused chiefly on correction. This modesty brings it into tension with the ambitions and optimism of the liberal state, the animating philosophy behind the American political project. And Americans are nothing if not optimists!

In fact, a state that exercises stewardly authority only, and is chiefly concerned with corrective justice, claims none of the traditionally democratic or liberal foundations of political authority, namely, consent, social contract, majority rule, and so forth. Democratic elections may still choose the governing party but Kuyper's state cannot claim popular sovereignty as its ultimate foundation. Kuyper pressed this point with secular as well as Christian colleagues because he saw in the popular sovereignty of the French Revolution the dark side of unfettered political authority in a fallen world. Not that he was unappreciative of the lighter side, too, because the rule of law restrained the forces of chaos. You have to have government and civil society. As he put it, "We have gratefully to receive from the hand of God, the institution of the state with its magistrates, as a means of preservation, now indeed indispensable. And on the other hand . . . we must ever watch against the danger which ever lurks, for our personal liberty, in the power of the state."[10]

I suggested above that Kuyper viewed the task of governors as chiefly corrective. There are older Christian themes at work here, harking back to the view of Augustine and other early Christian writers that a Christian prince was the preferred governor. Why a Christian prince? The expectation was that, with heavenly reward in view, he would act justly on earth and not yield to the lust for power. Kuyper, who was sensitive to the likelihood that any right to rule over others would quickly become the right of the strongest, conceived of human governing as essentially a dutiful responsibility, to be carried out in obedience to the ordinances of God, whose agent one was.

If you are forming the impression that Kuyper treated government as a special sphere, more problematic than the others, you have sound instincts! Politics for Kuyper was especially vulnerable to the rebellious acts we call original sin. Adam's sin was a "declaration of independence," a determination to marry knowledge to self-government and to dispense with God's higher law. In the social spheres, by contrast, which possessed natures more innate or spontaneous, it was as if he saw common grace more easily at work and effective. Politics is not like that. It is always something of a battleground between sin's effects and the sustaining power of common grace.

The other sphere that constitutes a battleground between sin's effects and God's grace is all too well known to each of us. Our own innate desire for liberty is elevated by obedience to God in the vocation he has for us. But always, contrary motivations are at work, too. Unlike the state, however, the individual person may come into a saving relationship to Christ. But whether in his innate quest for freedom or in obedient pursuit of divine vocation, the individual checks the tendency of the state toward despotism. And this, of course, Kuyper commended.

10. Kuyper, *Calvinism*, 81.

And so, from this brief summary of Abraham Kuyper's response to the risen King, we will draw a profound conclusion if we recognize government as essentially modest in scope, an obedient response to Christ our King, and concerned with earthly questions of sustenance, care, and justice. Politics is not about ultimate matters. Governments do not offer even the hope of final resolution[11] to any issue before them.

Conclusion

This summary is, of course, only a starting point. There is much more to Kuyper's perspective, forged as it was from a combination of political, theological, and pastoral reflection and experience. In the next chapter, I want to develop Kuyper's core emphasis on obedience as a political principle. I will do so by considering an unlikely source for a contribution to a politics informed by a Christian perspective. Usually associated with an apolitical posture, and often seen as preoccupied with personal holiness, the pietistic traditions reinforce Abraham Kuyper's chief priority for drawing up the scheme he called sphere sovereignty. His aim was to please God.

---

11. "Final solutions" properly send a familiar shudder down our spines as we recall the Nazis' efforts to eliminate the Jews.

Chapter 4

Pleasing God

WE HAVE TAKEN THIS exploration of the possibilities of Christian politics by first considering two major initiatives reaching back to the period following World War II. These were the Religious Right in the United States and the Christian Democratic Union in Germany. The Religious Right did not take the route of party organization but instead brought its own brand of social conservatism to the Republican Party and embraced in turn the economic conservatism of the GOP. The political activities of the Religious Right brought traditionally apolitical citizens into active engagement in American politics. Our second major initiative in Christian politics organized a political party on the foundation of Catholic social and political teaching. The CDU went on to play a major role in the rebuilding of Germany and continues to take a leading role in German politics.

We turned next to the theological foundations of Christian political engagement. In the last chapter I argued that the Easter message of Christ's resurrection provides the star from which to take our bearings for political reflection. In Jesus' willing sacrifice on Calvary, we learn what are the true characteristics of power. Power is made perfect in weakness. The Jesus who exercised true power by surrendering his life for the sins of the world, the Jesus who rose on Easter morning, is also the rightful King. What are the implications for politics?

We explored these implications in the writings of nineteenth-century Dutch statesman Abraham Kuyper. Kuyper held that government's task—in the sense of its calling or aptitude—is a positive but limited one. It is positive because there are unique tasks it must accomplish as an agent of the creator whose creation reflects norms of love, care, and justice. It is limited because *other* human agencies have complementary aptitude for love, care, and justice. Governments are not families. Businesses are not schools. So governments, Kuyper held, must make room for these other agencies to function and to flourish.

The Roman Catholic social teaching that influenced the development of the Christian Democracy we met in chapter 2 explains the role of government and of nongovernmental agencies in a similar fashion to Kuyper's. Government's *limitations* reflect God's purposes for nongovernmental human agencies. Those agencies, too, are divinely ordained and make their own unique contributions to human flourishing. Government's *obligations* include "wielding the sword" to protect society, punishing wrongdoing, and helping those nongovernmental agencies flourish in their own domains. Kuyper gathered these social functions and relations under the heading sphere sovereignty. The Catholic tradition speaks of the principle of subsidiarity.

All right, you may be thinking, constructing a "sovereignty chart" to explain how the Creator authorizes and empowers those human agencies that nurture and care for the creation is a pretty dry legal exercise! So let me make the same point but dress it in different clothing. It is time to consider the language of piety.

Piety and Political Conduct

Why did Kuyper undertake all the hard work of identifying the distinct responsibilities of families, churches, businesses, and governments and of distinguishing them from one another? His answer is clear: he wants to obey and thereby please God.

When we approach the question of the scope and limits of government through the lens of pleasing God, it is as if blood starts flowing along the arteries and veins of our legal chart, transforming it into a living organism. It may be that we are more used to thinking of pleasing God in terms of individual conduct. Honesty, integrity, responsibility, and accountability are what may come to mind. American culture reinforces this view because it treats ethics as chiefly confined to individual behavior. The Scriptures, on the other hand, always give ethical obligations a social dimension.

Kuyper insisted that divine revelation was essential for grasping the proper ethical "shape" of political life. "Sin makes futile every effort to found political theory on the observation of life and causes it to fail." But by that he did not mean that the Bible should replace observations from nature or the lessons to be learned from history. The Bible is not an instruction manual for politics. However, sin makes it hard for fallen human beings to read the "book of creation" and draw from it the wisdom and principles that would guide political life satisfactorily in a world not fallen. Holy Scripture functions like a pair of glasses—Kuyper's simile—"to read once again with (our) weakened eyes the partially obscured revelation of nature."[1]

In so saying, Kuyper makes Christian faith, which is necessary to accept the Scriptures as divine revelation in the first place, essential to understanding politics. For him it is the only way to get a proper grasp of the "ground rules, primary relationships, the principles that govern man's life together and his relationship to the most holy God." Again, this does not mean that Scripture lays down hard-and-fast rules for government as if the Bible were an instruction manual, nor does the Bible privilege one kind of political system over another. So varied are the circumstances under which nation-states exist, Kuyper observed, that Scripture permits a broad range of governmental types, including monarchy, commonwealth, and aristocratic republic, "as well as a democratic federation."[2]

Throughout these passages and others like them, Kuyper defers to God's holiness, love, and sovereignty. The sovereign God has made it possible for humans to cooperate with him, despite the fall. He appreciates that humans are stewards to the master, and will want to take their cues from him. God loves the world. He equips us to be good stewards. The Scriptures suggest principles to govern political life. Fallen though humanity is, Scripture is a source of norms that offer guidance for social organization.

Sphere sovereignty, then, should not be mistaken for a flat description of society as made up of different social functions with matching agencies, or for a prosaic statement of the obvious—a business is not a family and a family is not a government, for example. Instead, Kuyper devised sphere sovereignty to help us cooperate with God's good purposes in the domain of social and political life. To embrace it is, therefore, an expression of piety in the social and political domain.

It will be helpful at this point to turn to the Scriptures for further illustration. The Old Testament reminds us of the importance of ethical uprightness to the entire community, its purpose, and direction. The biblical law attaches considerable importance to justice in the most basic details of daily living. Consider Leviticus 19:36, "You are to maintain just balances

1. Kuyper, "The Anti-Revolutionary Program," 250.
2. Ibid.

and reliable standards for weights, dry volumes, and liquid volumes. I am the LORD your God, who brought you out of the land of Egypt." This verse contains a familiar juxtaposition of themes: a call to act with justice together with the larger reason for doing so. Justice in the use of weights and measures reflects the justice of God who is Israel's deliverer. To please and obey him, the Israelites are to uphold justice in their commercial relations, because these things, too, must reflect the justice of God. God's law, and Leviticus is the book of the law, extends to every domain of human life.

A different example reminds us that these standards come into conflict with Caesar's. When Pontius Pilate questions Jesus before his crucifixion, Jesus tells Pilate that his kingdom is not of this world, because if it was, "my servants would fight" to prevent him being handed over to the Jewish authorities (John 18:36). Pilate is completely baffled by this. He understands a political ethic that respects strength. The assertion that Jesus is King has to fit into that ethic. Jesus' evident powerlessness contradicts any claim to sovereignty as far as Pilate can tell.

Or consider Jesus's kingdom teaching as recorded in Matthew's gospel. The well-known passage, "But seek first the kingdom of God and his righteousness, and all these things will be added to you" (Matt 6:33 ESV), draws a contrast between worldly cultures and God's domain. Its full context deserves a brief outline. The episode in question has Jesus addressing almsgiving, prayer, fasting, treasure, and faith. Jesus begins by teaching that giving should not be showy, but private. He urges the same approach to fasting. He supplies his disciples the basic form of prayer to God the Father. He teaches that the attitude to treasure lays bare human motivations— where your treasure is, there will your heart be also—and he counsels his followers not to worry. It is in this culminating section that the quoted verse appears. We are to seek God's kingdom first and foremost because the very nature of God's kingdom is different from the world's cultures, whose standards, it must be said, come more easily to us! Jesus' teaching is challenging, then, for he teaches that once we have made God our top priority, "all these things"—daily bread essentially—will be given to those who have trusted God. This calls us to a distinct way of life, to God's goals rather than our own, a way of life that can only be oriented to the Christian hope by means of the exercise of faith.

But how might sphere sovereignty align with the power made perfect? Can organizations or agencies be asked to serve or to sacrifice? Are not individual commitments prerequisites for them? While this true, it may be said of natural institutions like the family or of a man-made one like World Vision or a pregnancy care center that its design and direction is toward good stewardship. Agencies like these establish a favorable setting or conditions for the responsibilities that their members will exercise. No family is perfect. Brokenness marks every human institution, natural or otherwise. But the examples just cited may still be turned toward obedience in reflecting God's good creation or in attempting to offer remedial care and justice in line with God's love for humankind.

Christian Piety, Natural Rights, and Republican Virtues

If concern with pleasing God should move us to a life directed to our hope in Christ by means of the exercise of faith—to a renewal of our minds, as St. Paul puts it—and if seeking first the kingdom of God calls us to an ethics of service and suffering, how will this ethical standard fare in the American political context? I want to consider two dimensions of the United States' political tradition that suggest two different answers.

A liberal democracy like the United States became[3] does not naturally encourage virtue. Take the most basic of democratic interactions, between a candidate seeking office and the voters he or she hopes will lend their support. As political scientist Benjamin Page once expressed it, candidates commonly invite voters into a simple calculus of "reward and punishment."[4] If I've done a good job, reward me; if my opponent has performed poorly in office, punish him (and reward me). The measure of performance is self-interest. How many times have you heard a presidential hopeful intone, "Are you better off today than you were four years ago?"

Now consider this definition of political corruption: using the power of public office for private gain. The "user" I refer to is not the candidate but the voter. Holding the office of citizen, voters are rarely offered an alternative to their self-interest as the reason to cast votes. Perhaps that's why John F. Kennedy's famous "Ask not you're your country can do for you, but what you can do for your country" stands out. Democratic election campaigns encourage citizens to use their voting power for private gain. Of course,

---

3. At its inception, the federal structure of the American republic loomed much larger than the rights of individuals or the democratic modes of election. But rights and majority rule have become much more prominent features.

4. Page, *Choices and Echoes in Presidential Elections.*

my vote's effect on political outcomes exerts only a fraction of the power wielded by a corrupt executive who steers government contracts into the coffers of a family business. But the incentives are usually framed in the same fashion.

One can imagine democratic campaigns in which the appeal to self-interest is balanced by other values, of course. But we should ask why that appeal is so rare. Perhaps we should not blame candidates or voters in the abstract but as unwitting consumers of the highly individualistic language we employ when "talking American," in a political or constitutional sense. What I mean is that the language and logic of our founding—you read it in the Declaration of Independence and the Bill of Rights—puts the individual center stage and devotes social and political authority to meeting his wishes. This is the "social contract." As the theory has it, individuals agree to give up just enough of their sovereignty to authorize government to act on their behalf.

But the chief weakness of our political rhetoric surely lies in the reluctance with which it grants government its authority. Where is the language of the common good? Where are the terms that describe "all of us" with approval? Where is membership? Deprived of such terms by the "bad guy" role government is obliged to play in the American drama—the role of setting limits to individual freedom—politicians trying to generate social solidarity usually resort to appeals to patriotism. Patriotic appeals have their place when the nation faces serious threats, but they become shop-worn very quickly from overuse. What's more, they can be downright mischievous, distorting political discourse at a deep level. If I wrap my policy preference in the flag, what I am saying to you who support an alternative policy preference? The opposite of patriotism is treachery. No wonder our political discourse is diseased!

It is important to take this excursion into the language we use to adjudicate political power and individual freedom because it is useful to contrast biblical ethics with the ethics American political discourse encourages. Biblical ethics is "social and transcendent," turned toward our relationship with God and other people. American political discourse is turned primarily toward defending individual liberty.

As Old Testament scholar Christopher Wright expressed it,[5] the big ethical question differs depending on whether community or the individual takes priority in one's vision of society. If *community* comes first,

5. Wright, *Living as the People of God.*

then the big ethical question takes the form: "What habits, dispositions, qualities, and skills must I acquire and develop to make my contribution to society as a fully functioning member?" The answer must then take shape in the language of *virtue*. We will have to ask how, and in what locations, character is best developed.

But if the *individual* takes priority in the conception of what a society ought to look like, then the big ethical question is bound to take a different form, something like, "How must society be structured and adjusted to maximize my liberty and enable me to reach my goals?" The answer to that question assumes a more familiar shape—we know it as the language of individual *rights*. In this setting, I am not obliged to develop a socially responsible character. Instead, society bears the obligation to make room for me to fulfill my desires: that's the highest value natural rights liberalism can conceive of. Modern societies, the American among them, chose this second question as the ethical question that should organize political life.

There's tension between biblical ethics and American political ethics when it's the liberal tradition of individual rights we have in mind. Their respective philosophical foundations share responsibility for the tension because it's so hard to reconcile them.

Of course, all is not quite as thin and bloodless in real life! Americans exhibit high levels of social support and charitable giving, and ordinary decency describes the treatment most Americans enjoy from our fellow citizens. What is not clear in the American case, however, is how far social norms should have to yield in order to accommodate individual rights if "push came to shove." In a strict sense, social contract theory pays little attention to society, because society is the product of individuals' choices and nothing more. In reality, societies like ours have cherished or accepted as given many features of traditional social connection and obligation. This is hardly surprising given the religious influences so formative of American ways of life.

Often, acceptance of customs has persisted relatively unexamined until someone issues a challenge on the grounds that a custom violates an individual right. Amid all the upheaval caused by lobbying for same-sex marriage in recent years, for example, it is easy to forget that the traditional norm of monogamous heterosexual marriage was theoretically open to challenge through most of the life of the Republic. But just because a challenge is conceivable does not mean that it will occur at the first opportunity.

Sociologist Charles Murray argues that certain social customs have provided essential support to the American political system. In his 2012 work, *Coming Apart*, Murray documents the course of social disintegration in the United States over several decades, tracing the practices of American citizens[6] in respect of four "founding virtues," as he calls them: marriage, industriousness, honesty, and religiosity.

These are embodied traditions generally amenable to Christian ethics, and not in tension with them as is the case for natural rights. And since they are embodied, their vitality or otherwise may be measured and the results plotted over time. Tracking the health of these founding virtues, Murray tells a sobering tale of a dividing society. Since the heady 1960s, the American elite, however bohemian in their youth, have swapped bohemia for relatively stable marriages, sound if overly supervisory parenting practices, impressive work habits, low crime rates, and at least modest levels of religious observance.

Not so their former neighbors. The "founding virtues" have all but disappeared from the bottom 30 percent on the income scale. Among these Americans, the percentage of married couples has slumped from just short of 90 percent to under 50 percent. Labor force participation has also slumped. Both violent and property crime, barely registering in the wealthy zip codes, have mushroomed among the poor. As for religiosity, it has declined across all sectors of the population, but the decline is much less marked among the elite, a fascinating inversion of the conventional wisdom.

Murray views the founding virtues and their accompanying practices and organizations as core components of social capital. Marked decline is serious, then. "It calls into question the viability of white working-class communities as a place for socializing the next generation." This, as much as the "new segregation" between rich and poor, sounds the alarm bells.

I suggest that Murray's findings have important consequences for Christian piety. Government's capacity to redress the decline of these virtues is largely confined to palliatives rather than cures. What I mean is that marriage failure multiplies the number of single adult heads of households, which in turn correlates with poverty and the need for offsetting government services. The long-term unemployed are also more likely to need government services. The police and criminal justice systems are called

---

6. As the subtitle, *The State of White America, 1960–2010*, indicates, Murray's focus is on white Americans. The purpose here is to demonstrate that the widely divergent attachments to the founding virtues do not follow but cut across racial or ethnic lines.

on much more frequently in areas of high crime; and declining religiosity (among other things) deprives people of sources of support, instruction, discipline, and solidarity, all vital elements of social capital.

That the founding virtues are social and not merely personal in nature helps to give Christian piety a broader grasp of its brief. To please God is as much a matter of collective as of individual virtue. Murray, who once confessed to the author he was a "soft libertarian," may give too much credit to these virtues and too little to the political structure built by the founding generation. But even the acknowledged father of the Constitution, James Madison, seems to have agreed with him: "To suppose that any form of government will secure liberty or happiness without any virtue in the people is a chimerical idea."[7] Murray's point, and presumably Madison's, too, is that the form of government the framers erected depended on the prior presence of certain virtues, ingrained as habits.

The presence of religiosity among Murray's founding virtues provides a link to the narrative we considered in chapter 1. The story of all the founding virtues corresponds to the story of the relationship between religion and democracy that we explored there. Just as in that account religion provided the moral code that freed democracy from the need to absolutize the natural rights, so the founding virtues in general similarly provide the social capital necessary to democracy's flourishing.

That they are now in steep decline is a crisis outside the competence of government to resolve. Government has to presuppose these virtues, if Murray and Madison are correct. It has to count on their already being there. Legal reforms may have contributed to their demise, but marriage, honesty, industriousness, and religiosity may at best only be encouraged by government action. They cannot be created. For the most part, their nurture depends on people's willingness to learn a way of life and to impart it to their children, to practice it in their homes, workplaces, and churches, and to be humble enough to learn from others and from their own mistakes.

Here is a distinct challenge for democratic government. Democracy is a notoriously impatient form of government, as battalions of former leaders will attest, having failed to grow the economy, prepare for a natural disaster, solve crime, and the like and then to have paid the price at the ballot box. Families and churches may be in a much better position to inculcate the founding virtues than government. But even they cannot achieve results overnight. Turn over "virtue education" to families and the results take time

7. Madison, quoted in Murray, *Coming Apart*, 129.

and they're hard to measure. Democracy and our constant campaigning simply won't wait and are impatient with measurement difficulties. America's democratic clock chimes every two, four, and six years, so democratic impatience is a fixture! And so democratic governments chafe at the need to share power, as Kuyper says they must share it, with nongovernmental institutions and agencies.

In the last two decades, presidential administrations have attempted to rethink government's relationship to nongovernmental providers of social services. Under President Clinton's reform of the welfare system, emphasis was taken off federal government provision and control of welfare services and placed on states and private groups as providers. To accommodate the latter, "charitable choice" standards were established. A social service provider could enter into a contract with government to provide services without risking its identity, mission, and standards—of particular importance if it was a faith-based organization. It was also important that faith-based providers could compete for government contracts without violating the separation of church and state. In the 2000s, President Bush extended charitable choice standards to a number of federal departments and agencies by executive order. This was the so-called faith-based initiative.

In an insightful analysis, Boston University law professor Linda McClain drew attention to a pair of highly revealing metaphors, employed respectively by Republicans and Democrats, to describe these initiatives.[8] The Republican language saw the faith-based initiative as an opportunity to "unleash armies of compassion," whose motivation and aptitude for providing services would fill the void that government was not suited to fill. Democrats agreed with the metaphor but kept government in the driving seat. They viewed the new initiatives as empowering government to "harness" private service providers. Thus the GOP framed sphere sovereignty in libertarian terms, as if government would have little to do once the private forces had been set free. Democrats, instinctively wedded to the view that government remains the chief and most legitimate agency of social change, in effect converted private social service providers into extensions of government.

8. McClain, "Unleashing or Harnessing 'Armies of Compassion'?"

Does the Political System Demand Certain Virtues?

Political scientist Amy Black approaches the question of virtues essential to the health of the republic in a manner that complements Murray's.[9] Where Murray argues America's political system relies on marriage, industriousness, honesty, and religiosity in order to thrive, Black focuses on the values that citizens and office-holders must adopt to ensure the effective operation of the constitutional system of separation of powers and checks and balances. Black's virtues—grace, humility, and reason—align well with the New Testament conception of power as made perfect in weakness. They also echo the classical-Christian formulation of virtues. From the classical world come the cardinal virtues of prudence, moderation, justice, and courage, to which the New Testament brings faith, hope, and love.

Black begins by developing her three as Christian virtues pure and simple, each attributable to a property of God or to created but fallen humanity. Grace, humility, and reason all express God's gift in creation. We enjoy God's goodness (grace), participate in the gift of reason as human beings at work in the world, and as such should embrace our status as creatures made in God's image, for we are not God (humility). All three help guard against sin. Despite its distorting effects, sin does not blot out God's grace. Reason helps fallen human beings check willful or passionate drives with facts and arguments. Humility checks the sinful tendency to put ourselves ahead of others or to defy God.

As she develops her argument, Black argues that these are virtues that serve the workings of the American political system. The three independent, but interdependent, branches of the federal government, along with the separation of federal from state government, call for compromise if the system is to function smoothly. Laws cannot reach the president's desk if House and Senate cannot agree. Absent compromise, the system can grind to a halt in an all-too-familiar gridlock.

Black treats compromise as a political expression of her three virtues. As she reminds her readers, strategic differences on policy matters are entirely normal in a free society, even among those who hold the same religious views. And she invokes both humility and reason as ways to create room for deliberation in advance of decision. Both serve, if I understand her correctly, as a counterweight to the ideological bent now distorting political discourse. Ideology usually imposes a simplistic template of values

9. Black, *Honoring God in Red or Blue.*

on politics and forces each and every issue into a binary frame. But issues are almost always more complex in their nature, history, and potential consequences—she cites the 1996 welfare reform legislation by way of illustration. With all these points, one can only agree.

A word of caution may also be in order. Black makes a strong claim about the demands of the political system when she writes, "People motivated by strong religious convictions can indeed have a significant influence on politics, but they must work within the confines of our pluralistic democracy."[10]

Should God or the political system call the shots? Is it a citizen's or a lawmaker's principal ethical task to lubricate the constitutional machinery so that the system's wheels turn smoothly—or is that to let this particular metaphor exert too much influence on our reasoning? Other considerations may be as or more important than smoothly functioning political machinery. If piety is a matter of pleasing God, then this will need placing ahead of smooth functioning—in some instances. Laws and policies that appear to violate Christian conscience, subject of course to careful examination of their particulars, deserve to be resisted. Practically speaking, compromise is only virtuous as a rule when its boundaries are made clear by the exceptions to that rule. Everything cannot be negotiable.

This discussion of Christian and republican virtues may never have been as important as it is now. From the Great Depression and the beginnings of the American welfare state to the 1960s and the Great Society social programs, American politics dealt largely in *economic* matters—on the domestic front, that is. Ideology drove foreign policy as the Cold War took hold and its distorting effects were felt far and wide, whether in the McCarthy hearings, or in the choices the US made to support particular regimes. Economic questions possess an important feature that helps them meet the demands of the American separation-of-powers republic. Simply expressed, when disputes can be quantified and the numbers adjusted to satisfy both sides or at least to minimize dissatisfaction, reaching agreement is relatively easy. Negotiations for new contracts often begin with the two sides far apart, only for both union and management to trade concessions as negotiations proceed, with agreement being finally reached. Legislators operating under rules that call for building coalitions of support in our divided system can build those coalitions successfully when they, too,

10. Ibid., 35.

have room to add, subtract, or modify the components of a bill to satisfy their colleagues.

But as political commentator and former Republican strategist Kevin Phillips noted several decades ago, American politics underwent a sea change in the 1960s, as civil rights came to the fore and infused our political rhetoric with the language of absolute rights—a language decidedly resistant to compromise.[11] In a relatively short period, the language of rights moved beyond questions of political liberties and penetrated debates over welfare, education, and health care, pressing the case that citizens' access to these goods was also a matter of rights. You cannot easily quantify rights, find the "middle ground," or in fact pursue most of the strategies associated with my above example. And that's how it should be, given the nature of these fundamental rights. Present-day American politics is pervaded by a style of political engagement that treats almost all issues the way civil rights deserved to be treated.

Conclusion

In different ways, Kuyper, Murray, and Black all testify to the necessity of virtues for a healthy polity. Murray focused on nongovernmental practices and institutions that contribute to the health of the republic. Black concentrated on the political virtues that should accompany the check-and-balance structures of American government itself. And Kuyper offered a comprehensive assessment of relations between government and civil society.

I argued that consideration of the norms that should shape political life is consideration of piety. These norms articulate the basic human desire to please God. Pleasing God is, to be sure, a matter of personal uprightness. But I would prefer to say that while it requires no less than this, it includes much more. Life together, in family, community, society, and the world, calls for ethical attention to the organizations and organisms in which it is lived. Or to reverse the saying, while living well in family, community, society, and the world is not confined to exploring the scope and limits of government's task, it does require that we explore these things.

11. See the narrative of the relationship between Christianity and democracy in chapter 1, where the arrival of these kinds of issues contributed to the breakdown of Heclo's Great Denouement.

Chapter 5

Balancing Act

The Role of Prudence

"THE LAND OF THE free . . . because of the brave." Even the uncertain calligraphy on the homemade sign along the roadside lent that lapidary truth a certain dignity.

The highway from Grand Junction, Colorado, going south passes through one All-America City award winner after another, from the farming towns of Delta and Montrose to the old mining town of Ouray, and over the passes to Silverton and Durango, and it was spectacular on a bright day of breathtaking colors in the fall of 2013. The neat red, white, and blue signs describing the awards, as well as the homemade ones displayed outside residences and businesses, advertised a determined commitment to family, home, and civic responsibility—a clear-eyed embrace of the links between liberty and sacrifice.

But in October 2013, Congressional Republicans had refused to fund the government, closing federal offices, national parks, and more. So, all was not well in this corner of the Rocky Mountains. "We the People . . . are p----d off," declared another patriot's cardboard protest. Variously expressed, the sentiment was widely shared. And though it threatened to dissolve into partisan acrimony in the next breath, the universal nature of disdain for the government shutdown and the style of politics it reflected deserve our attention. Citizens everywhere gave vent to similar frustration. Democratic elections theoretically empower them. As one-time presidential candidate Ross Perot declared in 1992, "they—the politicians—work for you!" Theoretically empowered as they are, somehow the people lack the tools to bring our representatives to heel. October 2013's government shutdown only underscored their impotence.

Constitutional checks and balances have always promised to secure minority interests against majority power. Checks and balances were designed for policy disputes, however, not for stymieing core congressional responsibilities for government's functioning, let alone for threatening a default on the country's debt obligations.

All this began to change with the government shutdown orchestrated by then-Speaker Gingrich in 1995. Two decades of increasing party polarization have obliterated any remaining barriers of Congressional decorum, which, like all forms of etiquette, is a kind of trust. Cliché though it is, crisis politics has become the new normal. Even when agreements are reached, they merely postpone another reckoning by creating new deadlines at a future date.

Change in the electoral system could solve some of these problems, perhaps, but the problems lie deeper than the rules governing elections. Ideologically driven politics threatens to convert every issue into an ultimate issue, on whose right resolution, supposedly, hangs the future of civilization itself! Wrap this high-stakes struggle in faith or the flag, and you have a political style as all-American as apple pie. It is a style we could all do without.

Paradoxically, Christians can choose to make things worse, or they can offer a partial remedy. Apolitical as most American Christians have tended to be, their return to the political arena in the 1960s—discussed in chapter 3—to defend the moral absolutes they saw to be at stake in the school prayer and abortion debates helped shape the polarized politics of today. So, too, it should be noted, did liberalism contribute to this style of politics with similarly uncompromising attitudes, as the abortion disputes again illustrate.

The partial remedy I have in mind is this. If Christ is King, and his power is made perfect in weakness, then we who follow Christ must refuse to deploy politics in search of ultimate solutions. If *Christ* is judge, *we* cannot look to the political process to secure a final judgment. Before we challenge our representatives to step back from this kind of politicking—and we should challenge them—we should make sure the lesson has sunk into our own consciences. No Christian should demonize the president, however strongly the two of them disagree.

In short, politics and government are not about ultimate solutions. They are about living in the fallen world, restraining evil, pursuing justice, seeking proximate solutions that respect human dignity, and helping non-governmental agencies make their own unique contributions to human flourishing. To be a Christian citizen is to contribute to stewardship of the creation, stewardship done in the hope of the new creation. But it is Jesus Christ alone who, "by his one, perfect, and sufficient sacrifice,"[1] will usher in the new creation. Politics and government do not secure or deny salvation. They do not bring the kingdom.

It might be easier to reach political agreement if political disagreement were not treated as evidence of treachery and one's own convinced positions were not placed on a par with divine revelation. This would be one political message worth hearing from America's pulpits![2]

Our subject matter is prudence.

Prudential decision-making—balancing ethical principles with unique circumstances—needs our attention because it is a constant feature and challenge of the fallen world. If Christian principles must always confront the unique circumstances of a world in rebellion against the rightful King, how is it possible to craft a politics informed by Christian understanding at all? To put it another way, does *this* facet of Christian understanding—that humans are in rebellion against God, and that creation "groans" as it awaits liberation from sin's effects—make a truly *Christian* politics an impossibility? Does sin place major or only minor restrictions on the possibilities for political action consistent with kingdom standards?

Consider Luke 14:31-32 (ESV), "Or what king, going out to encounter another king in war, will not sit down first and deliberate whether he is able with ten thousand to meet him who comes against him with twenty thousand? And if not, while the other is yet a great way off, he sends a delegation and asks for terms of peace." Jesus employed this example when urging the disciples to count the cost of following him. He slips it in, I think, with the expectation that heads will nod in agreement, that this is something everyone knows. You know your obligations but you must still count the cost, right? We all need to count the cost as part of living life under our various sets of circumstances. This is the language of prudence.

As we saw in the last chapter, Amy Black argues that grace, humility, and reason ought to characterize Christian political engagement. But let me revise her focus on compromise, to emphasize the process (negotiating or bargaining) over the outcome (compromise). Why the shift? Politics

---

1. This phrase is taken from the Anglican *Book of Common Prayer* and appears in the service of Holy Eucharist, Rite One, in the prayer titled, "The Great Thanksgiving."

2. A version of this introductory section appeared as "No Ultimate Political Solutions."

involves a series of bargains only some of which lead to the compromises Black and others approve. I say "others" with a wide range of democratic theorists in mind. Kenneth Minogue, for example, offering a verdict on the rise of the modern state, characterized its principal aim as the "accommodation of interests."[3] Bargaining often ends with parties walking away without the handshake that concludes a deal. There are many reasons for this. Sometimes the bargains were entered in bad faith. Sometimes, one party concluded that its interests could not be met by the proposed bargain, or could not be met at the time it was proposed. On other occasions, differences appeared to one or both parties to be too deep to resolve once the issue was being thoroughly explored.

To evaluate a political system only or largely on account of how productive it is, or what level of output it achieves or how smoothly it functions, is to surrender to an unhelpful measuring stick. Notice that the parameters of democracy encourage this kind of evaluation. They encourage the view that government's only task is to accommodate people's interests, wishes, and demands. Merely translating public opinion into public policy is not what even the American framers—with their commitment to individual liberty and their selective use of democratic procedures—had in mind, however. It is hard to square an emphasis on productivity with the framers' expectations that government would act in a restrained manner. It is hard to match their anxieties about the abuse of power to a commitment to legislating popular wishes.

The framers of the Constitution had a more modest goal in mind. They used democratic procedures to steer public officials toward acting in the public interest. Elections by the people served that end for the House of Representatives. But they were not considered appropriate for the Senate, which was elected by the state legislatures, or for the president, who was elected by the Electoral College. And as for the Supreme Court, presidential nomination and senatorial confirmation replaced elections altogether. The language that describes how judges maintain a right to their offices may best reflect the framers' overall wish, that all federal office-holders would discharge the duties of office, "during good behavior."[4]

On that basis, there simply isn't enough evidence to conclude that the Constitution's framers wanted the new government to be a well-oiled

---

3. Minogue, *Politics*. Interestingly, Minogue contrasted this modern aim with aim of classical and early Christian politics, namely, the right ordering of society.

4. Article III, Section 1.

policy engine, committed to maximum productivity with a minimum of holdups. For that one would have to weaken the instruments of check and balance—separation of powers, a bicameral legislature, and federalism— to give elected majorities unobstructed headway. And if you did that, the American political system as we know it would disappear.

When Democrats and Republicans cannot reach agreement, they should agree to disagree and emphasize the areas of common ground. As several recent crises—over the debt ceiling, the deficit, the "fiscal cliff," and the sequester, to say nothing of that government shutdown in the fall of 2013—demonstrate, citizens suffer considerable inconvenience and injustice when disagreements in one area forestall potential agreements in others.

Americans were subjected to ideological gridlock in 2013 when Republicans, urged on by the Tea Party wing of their party, shut down the government in a ploy to defund the Affordable Care Act. Ideology can suck all the oxygen from congressional debate over other issues. Should fruitful bargaining on immigration or gun control or prosecution of sexual assault in the armed forces have to suffer because a polarizing issue like this grabs center stage? Ideology is a lazy person's litmus test, the enemy of ordinary human reasoning. Ideology can be like the cowbird that lays its eggs in the nests of other birds. When the egg hatches, the fledgling then evicts both eggs and nestlings and insists on the exclusive attentions of the parent birds. The reasonable demands of other issues cannot be heard when ideology plays cowbird.

To their credit, Congressman Paul Ryan and Senator Patty Murray showed another face of prudence when they assembled, and won support for, a two-year budget deal in December 2013. Fatigue, concern over fallout in the 2014 elections, and the ambivalent public image of the Republican Party all helped create conditions in which a compromise budget, unimaginable a month earlier, could emerge. Member after member, stepping up to give the package his or her support, declared it far from the ideal budget they would have liked to pass. But pass it they did.

Ryan and Murray acted prudentially, seizing the moment when the counterproductive activities on the Right had backfired and elections loomed in the next calendar year. That is why one can debate the same issue on two different occasions and have radically different outcomes. Prudent negotiators can take advantage of changing contexts.

Christians should learn to recognize bargaining rather than compromise as the real constant in politics. Few if any political issues receive final resolution. Even the best-run program that meets today's needs may not meet those of the next generation. As responsible representatives address those needs, scarce resources will always be involved. And because they will be, so too will moral reasoning be involved. How much should taxpayers be expected to invest in programs that will not directly benefit them? How will that investment affect the availability of resources for other programs with equally legitimate, and thus competing, claims? And so on. We can contemplate all this much more calmly and carefully once we have accepted that politics was never supposed to reach final resolution.

Bargaining involves our interests, of course. But it also calls for our best judgment, too, for a listening ear, and for a willingness to defer judgment until the relevant facts have been identified and presented. Grace, humility, and reason are all at a premium. The skills more directly related to the process of bargaining are at a premium also. If ever there were an example of how best to take up Jesus' command to be wise as serpents, innocent as doves, this is it. Bargain well. Learn how. Know what you possess as bargaining chips. See if you have the numbers to move forward with your plans. Ask what those numbers represent. Weigh the costs and benefits of getting less than you seek. Understand your opponent. Try to reach agreement. Exercise patience.

Powerful forces work against the search for common ground. Putting the emphasis on reaching agreement violates the norms of campaign advertising because agreement generates fewer campaign donations than crisis does. Often, outside groups are responsible for perpetuating polarization. So we are stuck with groups that tout their unique capacity to Stop Hillary! or its equivalent.

The Power of the Sword

Few public officials can feel the sober responsibilities of office at greater depth, one imagines, than the governor facing a plea to commute a death sentence, or the president going to war who knows that his word will result in death and destruction with more certainty than it will secure the objectives sought, however good the preparatory intelligence and however justified the decision itself. In matters of criminal justice and waging war, governments wield the power of the sword, to paraphrase St. Paul, as a basic task and responsibility (Rom 13:4). In both cases that task is the stuff of life and death, justice and prudence.

It will be helpful to begin by noting a misunderstanding related to government's use of force. While the deployment of military force is a drastic step and should be a last resort, as is discussed below, the violence it unleashes is only the most serious form of the coercion exercised by governments all the time. All governments resort to coercion, even if they do so under the rules of due process and with a range of alternatives to consider, from financial penalties to incarceration. The legitimacy of governments—democratic governments no less than dictatorial ones—depends on the availability of sanctions to enforce the laws.

Resort to the responsible use of the power of the sword is, in this sense, no rare or distant occurrence, but an everyday one, calling for prudential judgments on a regular basis. For that reason it should be understood as a tool of public service for the common good, to be used by those properly authorized and held accountable under the rule of law. If we think of the power of the sword this way, we set it in proper context, and are best placed to consider its most challenging uses.

We live in a fallen world. In theological terms, sin marks each of us. Governments are all the better for being democratic, for enabling citizens to organize and articulate their interests, their convictions, and their wishes for society—as has been argued throughout. Although democracy is the best available setting for ensuring that necessary coercion is not "cruel and unusual," as the Eighth Amendment has it, coercion will remain necessary. It is not going to be replaced by democratic agreement.

In international relations, the theory of just war, with its origins in Christian writers like St. Augustine and St. Thomas Aquinas, provides a framework for the use of force by governments. A framework is not a cookbook, however! Those new to the theory will search in vain for a simple formula that gives a green light to some conflicts and a red one to others. What the theory does is raise key questions that must be considered before governments exercise the power of the sword. Answering the questions is not always easy, and initial answers usually pose other questions or raise possible qualifications to those answers, but the questions provide important guidance all the same. A brief summary follows:

Is the body waging war a legitimate one? The power of the sword rests with governments, not groups or individuals. War should never be a means of resolving private disputes but should only be exercised by legitimately constituted authority. Right away, you will see that this key principle raises important questions about legitimacy. Can democratically elected governments lay a stronger claim to this legitimacy than nondemocratic ones, for example?

Is the decision to wage war the only remaining alternative? Have all the others been exhausted? Is the war's goal limited to righting a distinct wrong? The easy case here is a war waged to defend against actual attack—those are always considered just wars. Again, however, the follow-up questions swarm: can a preemptive action that anticipates a direct attack fall with the standard? When preparations designed to deter an attack result in a dangerous escalation of tensions, and in some sense provokes the attack, is the justice usually attached to defensive war compromised? Doubtless the reader will add many other questions to this list.

Is success achievable? One can't get more prudential than that. And yet this is also a troubling question—many a conflict has been fought against great odds to improbable but eventual success. Is the goal of the war the restoration of peace with justice? Is the use of force proportional to the goals and the probable cost in human lives? Is the war being fought in ways that avoid as much as possible the targeting of civilians?

The value of just war theory lies, I would argue, less in some imagined perfection or clarity and more in its capacity to compete with other justifications that human beings, fallen as they are, put forward. Pride, revenge, greed, economic self-interest, territorial ambition, and the like insinuate themselves into nations' thinking, and democratic leaders, always anxious to win the support of constituents, are no less vulnerable to appealing to these values than are nondemocratic ones—perhaps more so. Last but not least, the just war tradition in particular amply reflects the limited purposes of politics that prudential reasoning in general brings to the fore. Especially in matters of war and peace, of recurring violations of sovereignty that form part of a nation's folklore, the temptation to resolve an issue once and for all is strong. But the tradition's measured principles remind us of the limited ends of politics this side of Christ's coming again. In war, as in politics more generally, there are no final solutions. This is a lesson that everyone, Christians included, needs to take to heart.

This brief section has not sought to offer more than a sketch of the prudential approach in regards to government's use of force. Lengthy treatments on the subject abound. I have found the work of James Turner Johnson very helpful.[5]

---

5. See, for example, Johnson, "Just War, as it was and is" and O'Driscoll, "James Turner Johnson's Just War Idea."

If the dilemmas involved in the use of force and other forms of coercion remind us that prudential judgments are a permanent feature of political deliberation, we should also recognize that there is more to prudence than balancing principles against "realities." Prudence is an approach to politics in its own right, with strong theological foundations—hence my title for the section that follows.

Uppercase Prudence

In his letter to Christians in Rome, St. Paul urged his fellow believers to obey the civil authorities as exercising powers ordained by God. For all practical purposes, it should be emphasized, the civil authorities in question were the occupying Romans, the same authorities who put Jesus to death in full knowledge of his innocence, to please the rabble. St. Paul's instruction is given in full knowledge of Rome's complicity in Jesus' death: Obey the political authorities that crucified your king.

The New Testament deepens this paradox. When Pontius Pilate, Roman governor of Judaea, questions Jesus' authority, Jesus replies, "My kingdom is not of this world" (John 18:36 ESV). And he goes on, "if my kingdom were of this world, my servants would have been fighting, that I might not be delivered over to the Jews." But in the Letter to the Colossians we read, "For in him all things were created: things in heaven and on earth, visible and invisible, whether thrones or powers or rulers or authorities; all things have been created through him and for him" (Col 1:16 NIV).

The creator of all human political authorities is king in his own right, exercising his sovereignty without succumbing to the violent ways of those worldly authorities.

Challenging—impossible—though it is to live up to the King's standards, the standards equip Christians to make appropriate political responses. As political philosopher Sheldon Wolin explains, believers do not have to imagine an alternative to the regime they live under. They already possess citizenship in another political order. Jesus prayed that his disciples would be "in the world but not of it" (John 17:6–19 NIV). The New Testament teaches throughout that Christians should live as aliens in their earthly homeland.

You may be thinking that this New Testament emphasis on the importance of viewing life on earth as a sojourn looking to the "hope of glory" in the kingdom of God would have steered the majority of Christians into separatist communities. If so, you would be wrong. Separatist sects and communities abound throughout the history of the church, of course, but the vast majority of believers have developed ways of life that integrate Christian hope with service and evangelism, and with different kinds of cultural and political engagement. This practice was already sufficiently developed for the theologian Tertullian (circa AD 160–220) to offer a summary of the way of life Christians adopted in the pagan empire:

> Christians are not distinguished from the rest of mankind by country or language or customs . . . . While they live in cities both Greek and oriental . . . and follow the customs of the country . . . they display the remarkable and confessedly surprising status of their [own] citizenship. They live in countries of their own as sojourners. They share all things as citizens; they suffer all things as foreigners . . . . They pass their life on earth; but they are citizens in heaven.[6]

The themes of this book are easily found in the Scripture passages quoted above and are reflected in Tertullian's short summary. Christ is the rightful and coming King, whose kingship sets the standards for political authority in this world. To live in accordance with his sovereignty, Christ's followers have developed distinctive "liturgies" or ways of life and have engaged earthly authorities in distinctive ways. Many of Christ's followers have held the world "lightly," investing in its peoples and its concerns, but not the pretensions of its cultures and leaders. More of Christ's followers should have done these things. This course of action has involved extensive suffering.

Consider Jesus' famous confrontation with the Scribes and Pharisees over paying taxes to the authorities. His opponents thought they had cornered him. "Is it lawful, Master," they inquired, "to pay taxes to the Roman authorities?" (One can almost hear the subtext, "Yes, the Roman authorities, you know, the occupying power that has subjugated God's people, and exacted a heavy price for the privilege.") Jesus asks for a coin. "Whose image does this bear?" he asks. "Oh, Caesar's," they reply. And again, one can hear the implicit, "Gotcha!" If Jesus says "yes," then his status as Israel's savior is undermined. If he says, "no," then those same authorities will easily deal with him. Either way, the Messiah is finished.

But their glee turns to ashes. "Then render to Caesar the things that are Caesar's and to God the things that are God's," Jesus replies (Luke 20:20–26 ESV).

---

6. Quoted in Wolin, *Politics and Vision*, 100.

In these passages, the basic elements of uppercase Prudence reveal themselves. The true King, who is willing to die to free creation from the power of evil and death, and who is willing to die at the hands of Caesar's agents, declares that Caesar's rightful authority is contained in the power of God, the power made perfect in weakness. Both God and Caesar are to receive our allegiance, but Caesar does not escape from fulfilling God's purposes, whatever his motives.

It fell to one of the greatest of Christian scholars to weave the classic treatment of the relationship between this world and the next, between Caesar and his creator God. In *The City of God,* St. Augustine divided those who obeyed God from those who disobeyed him. The earthly city is driven by love of the world. So Augustine argues that earthly government, though divinely ordained, has only diminished capacities. Governments punish wrongdoing and can, to that extent, bring about order and peace. The justice that can emerge from the earthly city is somewhat rough but in its basic outlines it reflects the divine design.

Government, in this understanding, remains divinely ordained. Indeed, earthly governments reflect, however dimly, the grace of God in what they are able to accomplish because the punishment of wrongdoing and the maintenance of peace are benefits to human societies. But, as political philosopher Robert Kraynak puts it, Augustine's doctrine of "Two Cities" *desacralizes* government.[7] What he means is that no particular form of government earns the biblical stamp of approval, neither democracy nor monarchy. No particular form of polity is "ordained by God." The prudential approach to politics resists conflating the Two Cities into a single blueprint for organizing society. The prudential tradition stands against theocracy.

What's a Christian to do then? What's government for and *not* for?

The Balancing Act

The prudential tradition asks that we bring all Christianity's dimensions—its supernaturalism, its piety and ethics, and its view of persons and society—to inform one another in this fallen world. This was the approach taken by Reinhold Niebuhr in *An Interpretation of Christian Ethics* (1935), in which he sought to protect an authentic Christianity by invoking transcendence as the bulwark against capitulation to the spirit of the age. Culture's norms are ever present, so the Christianity that guides us

7. Kraynak, *Christian Faith and Modern Democracy,* 86–104.

must be an authentic one. Niebuhr challenged the Christian political initiatives of his day, from both left and right, summing up his critique bluntly and with precision:

> Among the many possible causes of this failure of Christianity in politics the most basic is the tendency of Christianity to destroy the dialectic of prophetic religion, either by sacrificing time and history to eternity or by giving ultimate significance to the relativities of history. Christian orthodoxy chose the first alternative, and Christian liberalism the second.[8]

For Niebuhr, orthodox Christianity failed to develop appropriate ways of thinking about politics and acting politically under the conditions of a fallen world because it was focused on Christian ethics in its abstract purity. Liberal Christianity suffered from a similar failure, not because it wouldn't think about the fallen world—Niebuhr accuses it of thinking of nothing else—but because it tended simply to insist that people behave in virtuous and cooperative ways, regardless of sin. "Liberal Christian literature abounds in the monotonous reiteration of the pious hope that people might be good and loving, in which case all the nasty business of politics could be dispensed with."[9] In response to these counterproductive approaches, uppercase Prudence, or the prudential tradition of Christian political reflection, offers a balancing act. Christians are citizens in the kingdom of God. Christian principles, which reflect God's standards, are absolute. We live in the fallen world. To sojourn here, it is necessary to balance the two. This balancing includes recognizing that earthly political engagement has no salvific dimension to it. It amounts to using God's good gifts—for even rough justice and even earthly peace are goods—with respect but with appropriate expectations, to care for the world God made and loves and will redeem and glorify.

Naturally, this uppercase Prudence dovetails with the examples of lowercase prudence discussed in the first part of the chapter. Even divinely ordained government cannot deliver complete resolution of political issues. Government is not the appropriate forum for seeking ultimate solutions. Government concerns itself with proximate solutions to issues that will remain with us for further treatment on another day. Your city may design and implement a subway or light rail system to ease traffic congestion and pollution; but in twenty years property values in neighborhoods with

8. Niebuhr, *An Interpretation of Christian Ethics,* 129.
9. Ibid., 56–57.

commuter rail hubs may have risen so much that a fresh set of congestion and pollution issues have emerged as citizens forced further out in search of more affordable real estate have imposed those costs on the environment and transportation infrastructure. Policy will need to be refreshed and refocused. The original policy may have succeeded. But it has had its day. And so it goes.

In general, uppercase Prudence views the world through the biblical lens to advocate a guarded approach to government. In the particular American case that we are concerned with in this book, lowercase prudence recognizes the importance of bargaining well to maximize fruitful outcomes in the American political system.

Conclusion

The prudential tradition, it has been stressed, is not one that needs accessing only occasionally, when a crisis strikes, for example. In a real sense, it is as permanently relevant as the world is fallen. It takes its place alongside the permanence of pleasing God, exercising by faith our hope in Christ, and giving Christ his due as the risen King.

I began this chapter reflecting on the government shutdown of 2013, how unnecessary it was, how much it annoyed ordinary American citizens, and how it reflected the tendency in our politics to treat ordinary issues as if they had ultimate significance, a pattern that also looms large, as we saw, in the context of war. Here lies an opportunity within the Christian community to right a wrong understanding of the role of government. If those in the pews each Sunday heard a version of that message preached to them—there are no ultimate political solutions—and if those in the pews embraced that truth, the next step would be to demand that political leaders and lobbyists cease and desist from framing political issues in this fashion.

To this point, I have not privileged one Christian perspective on politics over others, but have instead assembled a kind of composite perspective. That perspective asks the believer to have in mind, and perhaps hold in tension, several considerations, all pertinent to political activity. Christian hope, God's sovereignty and the way he exercises it, pleasing God, and acting prudently, all contribute to the larger perspective. What follows are three chapters putting these principles into practice in the American political and cultural arena.

Chapter 6 _____

Issues in Christian Perspective: Immigration and Education

THIS CHAPTER AND THE two that follow it aim to apply the composite perspective of the previous chapters to several issues of current concern in American politics. I have grouped these issues in pairs as representing three conditions with a chapter for each pair. First, I want to consider issues that already respond to efforts by lobbying and related efforts by Christian organizations. Next, I want to take up a pair of issues where Christian teaching appears to leave little room for maneuver but that instead brings Christian teaching into conflict with prevailing policy preferences. The final pair first introduces Christian perspective on the international political situation before returning to the vexed state of domestic politics to suggest reforms that may help bridge the ideological divide.

I have chosen the issues to offer some breadth in American politics and to illustrate how the composite perspective of the preceding chapters may be applied to address particular issues. Christian hope, the sovereignty of Christ, pleasing God, and acting prudently all contribute to the responses. I hardly need to say that the list of issues is not comprehensive. Many who read the chapter may wish that I had addressed other issues. To those readers, I suggest that the observations and advice offered on these six may serve duty more broadly. That, at least, is my hope.

Immigration Reform: Gathering Momentum

Now that the number of people crossing the southern border of the United States has declined sharply, the opportunity to pass comprehensive immigration reform has never been better. Much as conditions were favorable for President Bill Clinton steering welfare reform through a divided Congress in the booming economy of the mid-1990s, similarly favorable conditions facilitated comprehensive immigration reform following the 2012 general election. In the event, the Senate passed a bill but the House did not. Getting from opportunity to policy involves marrying the seemingly irreconcilable—thicker walls and wider doorways. Let me explain.[1]

US immigration policy, Clark Cochran and colleagues explain,[2] has always reflected official constraints, despite the cultural perception of a "nation of immigrants." Puritan norms of religious compatibility led to limits being imposed on new settlers to colonies like Massachusetts and Rhode Island, for example. For the first half-century or so of the United States' existence, few restraints applied, but in the 1850s a familiar theme made its appearance. How would immigrants from different cultural, religious, and ethnic backgrounds from the native population change the political culture of the republic? Would they change it for better or worse? The clustering of immigrant groups into urban locations and the strong association alleged between their presence and social problems like crime and civil unrest, fueled a powerful xenophobia, epitomized by such upstart parties as the Know-Nothings. Later in the nineteenth century, Congress began introducing quotas to limit the number of Asian immigrants, and in response to pressure from labor unions, passed the Contract Labor Law that forbade entry by those with work contracts, in order to protect American labor from being undercut by immigrants prepared to work for lower pay.

Passage of the National Origins Quota Act in 1924 linked permissible immigration to the size of ethnic groupings already in the country—and thereby discriminated against those groups underrepresented in the population. In the 1930s, the Depression halted the influx of would-be immigrants, while World War II and the upturn in the American economy after the war created significant labor shortages. In response, the 1951 Migrant Labor Agreement treaty between the US and Mexico, nicknamed the Bracero Program, created a temporary worker arrangement, which lasted until 1964. President George W. Bush tried without success to revive it in 2004 and also failed to move more comprehensive immigration reform.

1. I have written on all of the issues addressed in this chapter, chiefly for The Center for Public Justice's *Capital Commentary* publication. Those commentaries form the backbone of the analysis of each of the chapter's subsections. The originals, together with current commentaries may be read at www.capitalcommentary.org.

2. Cochran et al., *American Public Policy*, 405–34.

Meanwhile, the xenophobia that had shaped early immigration laws had given way to a preference system focused on prioritizing those who qualified for legal immigrant status. The 1965 Immigration and Nationality Act established numerical limits that favored unmarried children of US citizens, spouses and children of permanent residents, professionals of various kinds, children and siblings of US citizens, needed workers, and refugees. Revised in the Immigration Act of 1990, current law is still based on its principles.

Laws passed in 1986 and 1996 were designed to address the growing problem of illegal immigration, especially across the southern border with Mexico. The 1986 law granted temporary amnesty and resident status to illegal immigrants with four continuous years of residency, but imposed penalties on employers who knowingly hired those here illegally. In the 2000s, monitoring of workers through the E-Verify system was established, while state laws variously granted to or withheld driver's licenses from the undocumented, or permitted their children to attend state colleges. The administration by executive order suspended deportation of the children of those here illegally.

Like health care, immigration has become a pawn in the ideological game. To date, comprehensive policy has proven elusive. Until the defeat in the 2012 Presidential election, Republicans made hostility toward paths to legal residency for the undocumented an article of faith; similarly, progressives have seemed unable to reconcile themselves to a robust legal regimen for discouraging illegal immigration. Remarkably, the Senate passed comprehensive legislation in 2013 that reconciled the two sets of priorities. The bill contained a path to citizenship, but also required border security to be certified before these provisions could take effect. No action occurred in the House, however, although Speaker John Boehner indicated willingness to see at least piecemeal reforms move to the floor in 2014.

Wider channels of legal immigration would also bring Arizona's and other states' recent efforts to discourage illegal immigration into proper focus. Just as important as the economic, social, and public justice benefits that accrue, wider doorways of *legal* immigration will increase the percentage, among those pursuing *illegal* entry, of those with criminal intent. The point of building thicker walls against illegal entry is to target those whose goal is not a better life, but terrorism, human trafficking, or the drug trade. If the wider doors can channel the legitimate refuge seekers and other would-be legal immigrants, then the higher walls can concentrate on those with nefarious or other illegitimate motives for entry. That's a view from 30,000 feet, of course. But it identifies the contours of a just policy.

A broad coalition of evangelical groups presses for immigration reforms. Representative of these is the Evangelical Immigration Table, which brings together under one "umbrella" a number of evangelical Christian organizations, church, and civic leaders. The EIT presses for comprehensive reform. Even more significant, perhaps, is the renewed interest among Christians with ties to the Republican Party. Consider the *Wall Street Journal* editorial in April 2014 authored by Ralph Reed of the Faith and Freedom Foundation and Russell Moore, president of the Ethics and Religious Liberty Commission of the Southern Baptist Convention. Reed and Moore refer to immigration reform as a "moral imperative" and identify several principles that they believe could form the foundation of a conservative approach to immigration.[3]

They argue that a principled Christian policy should rest on "the rule of law, security and safety, family unity, and human dignity." And they call for policies to keep families together, substantially expand H1-B visas for skilled persons, and provide safe and legal work opportunities for those who enter the United States legally. They reject favorable Republican poll numbers going into the midterm elections as justification for the GOP's foot-dragging on immigration reform.

Hard as it is to argue against success—Republicans won big in the 2014 midterms—the GOP exposes itself to both ethical and political peril by doing nothing. As the party of limited government and market forces, Republicans risk defining themselves as the party of No—especially six years into resisting an activist Democratic administration. The downside of playing up the market and playing down the government is that it can project an image of society on autopilot, with government's role reduced to plugging in the right coordinates for the final destination.

Such a vision is apt to induce queasiness for the anonymous citizen in seat 41E! Those at the helm need to be engaged and proactive, whatever their convictions. The moral imperative generated by the needs of democracy itself is to draw citizens into political debate by outlining options, offering alternatives, and encouraging responsible choosing.

Reed and Moore are right to point to probable electoral success in November as an ethically unacceptable reason for deferring action on

---

3. I discussed the Reed/Moore editorial originally in "Simply Because It's the Right Thing To Do."

immigration. Their call for a conservative approach to immigration reform, together with their appeal to a Christian view of human dignity, is welcome, as much because it is conservative—and lots of resistance has come from that quarter on immigration—and more because it promises to engage the debate with specific policy items linked to principles. At the same time, their position remains symptomatic of the ambiguous application of values to public policy initiatives.

These proposals for immigration reform display an imbalance tilted toward burdening the undocumented. Those here illegally would be required to pay fines and back taxes, admit wrongdoing, learn English, submit to background checks, and demonstrate their ability to support themselves, all in the name of human dignity—of the *imago Dei*. But if human dignity is to be invoked in support of these actions, doesn't it also call for guarantees of permanent residency and security from deportation? Or do the political calculations persist in extracting their pound of flesh?

"The House should pass legislation that reflects conservative values of strong and secure borders, the rule of law, economic opportunity, and strengthening of the family." This proposal begs a question: Must border security be certified before the other elements are implemented? More specifics would have helped.

While the Reed/Moore proposal raises as many questions as it addresses, its strictly moral appeal for action on immigration is welcome. It is refreshing to hear a call to action simply because it is the right thing to do. Although Christian perspective may range widely on issues like this, the common ethical frame of reference can help discover common cause.

Education Policy: Jefferson vs. Kuyper?

In 1922, the state of Oregon passed by ballot initiative an amendment to its compulsory education law. The amendment eliminated the exemption for children attending private, religious, and military schools in the state. Major sponsors of the ballot measure included the Ku Klux Klan and the Masonic Grand Lodge of Oregon. Their undisputed target was Roman Catholic schools. The measure won passage with nearly 53 percent of the votes cast. Now every Oregon child of school age had to attend public school.

Before the amendment went into effect, however, it was challenged by a military academy and by a Catholic religious order that operated parochial schools. The state lost and appealed to the US Supreme Court. When the Supreme Court of the United States heard the case on appeal, it sided unanimously with the private schools.[4]

While *Pierce v. Society of Sisters* closed the door to government exercising exclusive control of elementary and secondary education in the US, the spirit of the Oregon law lives on in the widespread presumption that education is government's job. Despite Justice McReynolds's criticism that Oregon was treating schoolchildren as "creatures of the state," such a view has deep roots. Versions of that view live on in mainstream ideas guiding education policy to this day.

According to Thomas Jefferson, government-run schools were necessary to the ethical health of the new republic. Jefferson and his much younger contemporary and leader of the Common School movement, Horace Mann, conceded that homes, churches, and private schools provided moral training. But such training by private institutions was not enough for them. What those institutions could not do was nurture republican virtues.

As political scientist James Skillen explains,[5] Jefferson was eager to liberate republican citizens from various prejudices encouraged by arbitrary authorities, chief among them clergy. In Jefferson's opinion, they "tyrannized" people's minds. Common education would free people from this tyranny and develop in ordinary citizens a sense of the common good. As Jefferson conceived of the forces in play, on one side lay sectarian, private, and parochial forces; on the other nonsectarian, common, and universal ones.

Jefferson's view of society bore little resemblance to Abraham Kuyper's. Unlike Kuyper's conception—a differentiated society comprised of various human agencies, both governmental and nongovernmental, each with its vital role to play—Jefferson's viewed society as a social contract among free *individuals*. In the Jeffersonian conception, family could not be thought of as a necessary agency for the education of society's members, but was treated as a parochial force, whose tendency to reinforce sectarian values had to be overcome by a power that could inculcate universal values. Only the state could achieve this.

---

4. *Pierce v. Society of Sisters* (1925) looks like a religious liberty case, and the Sisters' lawyer did challenge the law on the grounds that the First Amendment freedom of religion prevented the state from exercising exclusive control over education. But at that time the Court had not decided that the First Amendment restricted *state* actions as distinct from *federal* ones. Instead of deciding on religious liberty grounds, the Court struck down the Oregon law for denying the private schools use of their property without due process of law under the Fourteenth Amendment.

5. Skillen, *In Pursuit of Justice*, chapter 6.

Jefferson found virtue in religion and supported religious liberty as a private right. But he regarded religion as unconnected to the purposes of the republic.

The staying power of such views in today's debates over school choice and charter schools ought to seize our attention. Considerable energy has been devoted to protecting the monopolistic instinct of American educational policy. The *Pierce* case, we should remember, came toward the end rather than the beginning of the "school wars," waged by a Protestant culture against the demands of waves of Catholic immigrants who sought government support for Catholic schools. Some thirty-nine states adopted "Blaine Amendments" to prevent government funding of *any* religious school, with Catholic parochial schools being the principal target. *Pierce* attempted to go one better and drive even private religious schools out of business altogether.

At the time that the Blaine Amendments were passed, most public schools embraced a Protestant moral code, as we saw in chapter 2. Prayers and Bible readings were as common as the moral lessons taught by McGuffey Readers. Blaine Amendments did not proscribe moral teaching based on the ethics of the New Testament. Recall from chapter 1 Hugh Heclo's Great Denouement between church and state, Christianity and democracy. This was firmly in place at the time and it held sway until the mid-twentieth century. This was a position full of contradictions, of course. It tried to harvest Christian ethics from the soil of revealed religion without getting its hands into that soil and without allowing those it viewed as suspect sectarians— Catholics, chiefly—from sowing their tares among the wheat.

In the mid-twentieth century, a movement to separate church from state came close to recreating Jefferson's secular republic. Even in the *Pierce* case in 1925, as Skillen explains, the Jeffersonian view had won by default. Children should not be made creatures of the state, the Court said, but the judges still treated the state as the principal agent for providing education. By 1971, in *Lemon v. Kurtzman*, the Court summarized a quarter century of strictly separating church and state with a famous three-part test for constitutionality. Laws involving religion would face strict scrutiny from the courts but could pass muster if their secular purpose was clear and the aid to religion incidental; if they neither advanced nor retarded religion; and if they avoided "excessive entanglement" of church and state. Like almost every other religion-related case in that quarter century, the subject matter of *Lemon* was education. Strict separation only reinforced the default view that government alone possessed unchallenged legitimacy in the field of elementary and secondary education.

As it turned out, however, *Lemon* was a high-water mark for strict separation. Succeeding decades have seen that tide ebb somewhat. A growing private school movement with religious schools leading the way, and a quite unanticipated homeschooling movement strongly embraced by Christian parents seeking better options for their children, challenged the status quo. Within the public schools, school choice voucher programs and charter schools emerged. School choice programs allow parents the option, under certain conditions, of moving their children to a different school district in the public school system. Charter schools are public schools whose principal feature is the greater power they give to school administrators to adopt new programs and to hire and fire teachers on the basis of performance. The courts have validated school choice and voucher programs even where these permit parents to select religious schools for their children. Indiana has gone further than most other states in this respect. It is now three years into a voucher program that allows parents the choice of alternative schools, including private religious schools. The program has quintupled enrollment since its inception.

What does all this mean? The United States may, by fits and starts, be moving away from the Jeffersonian model toward a pluralistic educational system. In Skillen's judgment, this is desirable. He thinks there should be an open market in education. Schools are for schooling, not for promoting public secularity. They should not be used to confine religion to the private sphere. All schools are "public schools," in that they educate the children of society.[6] They should do so not in competition but in cooperation with the primary agents in education—parents.

Justice in education means equal treatment of world views rather than privileging one of them, even if a view like Jefferson's enjoys a long history and still enjoys widespread appeal. While American culture may exhibit changing attitudes toward different world views—changes that many Christians describe as secularizing trends—active preservation of the liberty of parents to select schools they think are appropriate for their children ought to be the principle governing policy. Now that government is so heavily involved in raising revenue to distribute for schooling, there

6. For a Roman Catholic perspective, see Boffetti, *All Schools are Public Schools*. Boffetti argues that the state may enhance the overall quality of its education by aiding these schools and generating competition, which has been shown to produce higher achievement scores in all the state's schools.

are no defensible grounds for confining spending to one kind of school on the fiction that public schools best represent the universal values of American society and thereby justify giving government a rightful monopoly of legitimate educational choices. Justice is best served by formulas that allow tax revenues to follow the choices parents make.

Education is a many-sided issue. The focus on religious liberty and parental primacy does not exhaust these any more than it gives voucher programs immunity from unintended consequences. Indiana's statewide voucher program is a case in point. It began as a program to provide choice to parents from low-income backgrounds, giving them a measure of liberation from failing inner-city schools. According to the *Indianapolis Star,* however, by the third year of the program, the majority of the 20,000 children taking advantage of the voucher never attended a public school in the first place and come disproportionately from suburban districts rather than urban ones.[7] Critics warn that the program may in time create a two-tier system—underfunded public schools and voucher-assisted private schools, both funded by Indiana's tax revenues. Perhaps the moral of the story is that as long as such programs merely retrofit existing public school systems without replacing them, that outcome is a likely one. This is a difficult debate and will need much wisdom in finding just resolution. Does choice matter more to parents even than proven quality? That is a complex question. But we can say that, for parents, control over which schools their children will attend is a key factor in securing quality education.

The larger point I want to make by deploying the example of education policy is that it has proven responsive, from state to state, to ideas informed by Christian perspective. This is hardly surprising, of course. A complementary set of motivations has propelled believers to undertake one educational innovation after another through the nation's history. Most of America's four-year private colleges trace their origins back to a founder or founders eager to provide education as a community service, or to train missionaries, or to strengthen the denomination in question.

The skirmishes along the border of church and state are often taken as omens of a dark future for Christian education. I think these are overly gloomy predictions. Education policy has proved responsive to Christian concerns and will continue to prove responsive to them. Here is an area of policy where Christian perspective can be a resource for educators of all stripes. Ironically, the composite of school choice, charter schools,

7. Wang, "Indiana voucher students double to nearly 20,000."

homeschooling, and voucher programs may even reacquaint progressive supporters of a government-run system with the virtues of liberty—choice, after all, is the watchword of progressives in almost every other area of social policy!

On that note, the hallmark of successful Christian engagement with a policy issue of any kind is that it opens fruitful alternatives for everyone, not just for Christians. So, for example, the goal of pursuing schooling options that allow Christian parents to have their children educated in a school aligned with their Christian beliefs should allow all parents to have their children educated in a school aligned with their beliefs—if that's something they want.

Conclusion

The succeeding chapters take up issues that in their American setting display less responsiveness to Christian perspective than the two discussed in this chapter. But let me make a general point about tackling all these issues.

In the United States, citizens and their representatives may address all kinds of social and economic challenges confronting society. Our political structures are orderly and open. These features amount to a blessing, for which our appropriate response is gratitude.

The circumstances of this blessing are laden with paradox. As I have noted earlier, the language and logic of the liberal tradition is at odds with the Christian tradition in important ways. To put it crudely, liberalism views society as a collection of individuals who have made a deal with one another. The Christian idea that society is a moral order containing norms—"oughts, dos, and don'ts"—is alien to the political theory of the United States. The cracks did not become gulfs because for many decades an unofficial but widely accepted moral code drawn from Protestant Christianity enjoyed sufficient support to prevent the conversion of American liberalism into a competing code whose "oughts, dos, and don'ts" would be backed by the force of law.

The consensus behind that unofficial protestant moral code has now largely collapsed. Now there is a growing tension between Christianity and democracy in the United States. That tension makes critical the quality of the "vehicles" Christians have turned to in order to navigate the political terrain.

Lacking a political party of their own, many (especially evangelical) Christians have aligned themselves with the Republican Party. In one respect, this has conferred real benefits. It has seated sympathetic representatives at the legislative "table." This is always the most helpful way to articulate your perspective. Win seats, and these will then double as votes to trade in support of policies. In this respect, party representation is superior to relying on lobbyists, because lobbyists remain in the lobbies! There is a downside—of course. Alignment with an existing political party identifies your group as supporters of all of that party's commitments. So Christians must weigh the cost of this strategy and take care to explain their political allegiances precisely. I will return to this point in chapter 9.

For all the blessing of the orderliness of the political structure, however, Christians still wage their campaigns with one hand tied behind their backs. The social contract terrain is philosophically alien to a biblical conception of humans and society; and the lack of a political party of their own makes forging alliances problematic and bargaining with opponents very difficult.

And yet, I think, Christians in the United States should see more opportunities than obstacles in the political system as presently constituted, more justice than denial of justice. They could do worse than view the legal struggles, debates over bills, and even acrimonious campaigns as a pretty good normal, not as one crisis after another, each threatening to overwhelm or put down people of faith. Engaging politically will inevitably invite struggle, debate, and acrimony. But, our prudential instincts ought to tell us, it's a normal state of affairs one must engage and not shrink from.

Chapter 7 _____

Issues in Christian Perspective: Abortion and Gay Marriage

Abortion and the Role of Government

ON THE EVENING OF October 11, 2012, Vice President Joe Biden and Congressman Paul Ryan sat down with moderator Martha Raddatz for the lone debate between the candidates for Vice President. The debate provided important insights into the candidates' positions on abortion. In particular, Raddatz asked these two Roman Catholics to explain the religious grounds for their positions.[1]

Vice President Biden confessed himself bound by the church's teaching that life begins at conception. But he was quick to insist that he could not impose this teaching on others of equally sincere moral conviction who reach different conclusions. Congressman Paul Ryan acknowledged the church's teaching along with the testimony of science and reason as the source of his convictions on the subject. For these reasons, he declared that he opposes abortion, but would provide exceptions for rape, incest, and threats to the life of the mother.

Missing from this exchange between two Roman Catholics was any reference to their church's teaching on the responsibilities borne by government concerning abortion. To be sure, Ms. Raddatz asked both candidates to consult their personal religious convictions for the contribution these make to their views on abortion and even pleaded with them

1. An earlier version of this opening section of the chapter was published as "Religion, Abortion and the Role of Government."

to speak "personally." Different though Biden's and Ryan's answers were, both remained trapped within this artificial constraint. Neither candidate contested the American-as-apple-pie separation of religion from politics that was implicit in the question.

What might these two Catholic candidates have said?

As the Center for Public Justice's *Guideline on Human Life*[2] holds, government is obliged to protect life and to protect the family as the primary life-giving unit of society. Government should also provide supportive conditions for the family, acknowledging that the family bears primary responsibility for the nurturing of children. Even in unusual or emergency circumstances, where pregnancy is unplanned or out of wedlock, the state's responsibility lies in that direction of support for the new family, rather than in promoting the availability of abortion on grounds of personal autonomy.

When the Supreme Court legalized abortion in 1973, it substituted the right of privacy as government's chief concern. It relegated government's responsibility to provide help to the family to secondary status at best. Help for the family can take the form, among other things, of pregnancy counseling, health care for the woman and her child, and adoption services. All of these contribute to a supportive environment in which a woman—be it a scared and isolated teenager or simply a mother who did not expect another pregnancy—considers her options. These services suggest that government's responsibility is a broad one. Justice would not be served simply by overturning *Roe v. Wade*.

All abortions are grave matters because each abortion destroys a human life. Is every abortion necessarily wrong, however? By considering the case of rape, a core principle may be distinguished. When a man and a woman have sexual intercourse and the woman conceives a child, the two of them have assumed obligations to the child and to each other. When the conception is the result of rape, the woman has not willingly set aside her own autonomy. In these circumstances, government may consider policy exceptions to the guiding principle of protecting life generation and the family life that sustains it, and those exceptions might include allowing some abortions.

The larger point about these arguments is that they are religiously grounded arguments—*about the role of government*—and they are the kind of arguments that Catholic teaching articulates with abundant clarity. Messrs. Biden and Ryan failed to do this teaching justice and thereby failed

2. http://www.cpjustice.org/content/human-life.

to enrich the important public discourse on abortion, sexual responsibility, and the protection of children and families.

US courts have embraced a very different set of values from the ones outlined above. From a biblical point of view, the courts have turned the core governmental obligation on its head. They have valued personal autonomy over the protection of persons. And even though state laws impose a range of restrictions on abortion (and in the case of so-called partial birth abortions outright prohibition), government continues to default on its primary responsibility.

What we can detect here is one dimension of the conflict between Christianity and liberal democracy discussed in chapter 2. The liberal tradition values personal liberty—autonomy and self-government are effective synonyms—to the exclusion of other values *when these other values come into conflict* with personal liberty.

Prudentially speaking, one would not predict major change in the courts' views of the rightness or wrongness of abortion. The Constitution they interpret is framed in liberal language and logic. Legislative restrictions on abortion have proved to be within reach without violating that language and logic, however. There is reason to believe that further restrictions may also survive legal challenges. But there is little prospect of altering the Constitution's core priorities. Liberty will continue to take precedence over care of persons.

There are alternatives to the legal and legislative approaches to abortion.

Emily Dickinson's frequently quoted advice is to tell the truth, but tell it "slant,"[3] and it serves to suggest strategy for approaching issues in the face of low probability that the law will change. It's a strategy that surrenders no principle but offers a constructive resolution.

The slant alternative to the law that permits abortion on demand as a dimension of personal privacy is to try to make the law moot. Even if Christians simultaneously campaign for government to amend, repeal, or overrule *Roe v. Wade*, this alternative is worth considering. The slant alternatives to abortion include expanding pregnancy care services and facilitating adoptions. The first is capable of reducing the number of abortions because it offers to surround the pregnant woman with people who can discuss her choices, inform her about other sources of help, and assist her in finding ways to discuss her situation with family and friends. Surely, no

3. Dickinson, "Tell all the truth but tell it slant."

one size fits all, but pregnancy care centers provide help that is humane, local, and engaged—the right sort of setting for the decision the woman does make. The second, similarly, undercuts the old arguments about unwanted children by raising the visibility of those couples seeking to adopt.

If would-be adoptive parents increased in number, the result could be to give the lie to the concept of the "unwanted" child. Initiatives along these lines could include lobbying public officials, of course, but here again the principal effort lies outside legal remedies.

In recent years, technological advances in ultrasound have detected fetal heartbeats very early in pregnancy—as early as six weeks, according to counsel defending North Dakota's version of such a law in 2013. States have fashioned laws that take this early date as the latest date at which abortions should be legal, in contradiction of the *Roe* standard, which approximates twenty-four weeks, or "viability," i.e. the time at which it is held that a fetus may survive outside the womb. "Admitting privileges" laws, a version of which was upheld in Texas in 2013, require doctors performing abortions to have these privileges at local hospitals.

Anyone taking a stand on abortion, whether in the form of protests and counseling outside abortion clinics or lobbying for changes to the law, ought to look carefully at the consequences of victory. If the issue is truly one of protecting life generation, then ending abortion does not mean that all the state's obligations are at an end also. In a significant, and certainly expensive, way, they are just beginning. Medical and social services ought to be made available to the new mother and child, and these should be provided with the same energy that the state resisted abortion on demand. Weighing the importance of these services, one will quickly find oneself balancing several sets of priorities all of which have implications for budgets and taxes. One hopes that Christians would put their efforts behind this more comprehensive approach and speak to its implications.

Same-Sex Marriage

Following the Supreme Court's decision in the summer of 2013 in two pivotal cases involving same-sex marriage, one political blogger headlined, "A home run but not a grand slam for gay marriage advocates."[4] At the time, I thought that verdict was about right. And in the process, I have suspected the institution of marriage has changed permanently, at least in its public

4. Howe, "A Home Run but Not a Grand Slam for Gay Marriage."

and legal incarnation.[5] With the decision of *Obergefell v. Hodges* in 2015, which required registrars to issue marriage licenses to same-sex couples, this suspicion appears to have been confirmed.

In the first case, *Hollingsworth v. Perry*, Chief Justice Roberts held that private citizens who supported California's Proposition 8—which banned same-sex marriage but was overturned in a lower court—could not appeal that ruling. State officials declined to defend Prop 8 so private citizens tried to do so in their place. But the Supreme Court ruled they could not bring a lawsuit because they could not show a direct "injury," so Prop 8 died.

Unlike those citizens who tried to defend Prop 8, Edith Windsor alleged a sizeable injury—$363,000 worth—and got her day in court by challenging the 1996 federal Defense of Marriage Act (DOMA).

In *U.S. v. Windsor,* the justices overturned a key provision of DOMA, one which defined marriage as a union of one man and one woman, because it did not extend the tax and related benefits of marriage to same-sex couples. Since DOMA's passage, several states now grant marriage licenses to same-sex couples. Windsor, as the surviving spouse of one of these marriages, sued to recover federal taxes she paid on her late spouse's estate.

The case got plenty of attention, especially because Justice Kennedy wrote that DOMA was unconstitutional under the Fifth Amendment's protection of a person's liberty. Unfortunately, he did not stop there. In widely quoted lines, he accused Congress of a "bare desire to harm"; of "demeaning" the choices of married couples and "humiliating" the children of same-sex couples. These motivations, he alleged, constituted the core purpose and effect of DOMA—even though no states conferred such marriage rights in 1996 when DOMA was passed!

Obviously, these two five-judge majorities differed markedly. In *Perry*, both liberal and conservative judges joined the Chief Justice in denying "standing" to Prop 8 supporters. The other four, again a mix of liberals and conservatives, would have allowed their lawsuit, which would have cleared the way to consider the constitutionality of same-sex marriage. On that question, they would have been divided, but who knows what the split would have been.

On the other hand, the judges disagreed in *Windsor* along conventionally ideological lines. The four liberal judges sided with Justice Kennedy, with the conservatives in opposition. Despite Kennedy's intemperate language, the majority crafted a narrow opinion. They only struck down

---

5. See Sherratt, "Same-Sex Marriage and the Power of Rights."

part of the law, confined their ruling to those states with same-sex marriage, and let stand DOMA's provision that states may not be compelled to accept as legitimate the same-sex marriage laws of other states.

Kennedy's ruling was not a *states' rights* ruling, even though this avenue was open to him. After all, marriage law has been, traditionally, a state matter, not a federal one. He preferred instead to emphasize the affronted dignity of persons inconvenienced by DOMA, not the power of states to regulate marriage. Why? Affronts to individual rights resonate legally and culturally by taking aim at any government that restricts them, state or federal. If Kennedy had used the right of states to shape marriage law as the basis for invalidating provisions of the federal law, he would have thereby upheld the sovereign power of those states that had not legalized same-sex marriage. Many of those states had enshrined the traditional one-man, one-woman definition in their constitutions. *Obergefell,* however, put an end to these initiatives.

What the Supreme Court eventually decided is hinted at in these two cases. In contrast to Justice Kennedy's emphasis on personal liberty rights, the Chief Justice acknowledged in the *Hollingsworth* case the rapid changes in public opinion over same-sex marriage, implying that state governments are competent to decide the issue for themselves. Roberts's ruling takes the long view and hints that legislative deliberation, not judicial fiat, should hold sway.

Would Roberts's preference for a decentralized and legislative resolution or Kennedy's universal rights-based resolution carry the day? Now we know. Marriage as we've known it has changed. Its new face is increasingly artificial and legal, and less natural and conventional.

Still, critics of these rulings are many. Former judge Michael McConnell, for instance, thinks opposition stems "from the fear that conscientious opponents will be victimized."[6] Justice Kennedy's ill-chosen words could incite both fear and victimization. They leave no safe ground for a conscientious opponent to stand.

Roman Catholic Archbishop Timothy Dolan also voiced a major criticism, that "the common good of all, especially our children, depends upon a society that strives to uphold the truth of marriage."[7]

6. Schulzke, "Supreme Court upends marriage debate."

7. United States Conference of Catholic Bishops, "Supreme Court decisions on Marriage."

His is a common criticism: that gay marriage deprives children, not of personal care and affection, but of the irreplaceable contribution to their welfare and development of either mother or father. Archbishop Dolan's criticism presumes the essential and complementary differences men and women contribute in marriage and child rearing, but this presumption is not shared, and probably cannot be shared, by the court in reference to the language and logic of the Constitution.

Why would I make this assertion? It is the way these two rulings reflect core values of the American Constitution that ought to grab our attention. The Constitution describes individual liberty in elaborate detail but has little to say about natural and social agencies. So, for example, by the Constitution's logic, the environment does not possess its own integrity. No, it's just someone's property—which government may not seize without just compensation and only by following the due process of law.

We should not be surprised, then, to discover that tradition or convention, let alone an appeal to natural law, prove no match for individual rights like equal protection or due process. Marriage has acquired over many centuries certain features from tradition and convention, and woven into these, of course, is religious understanding. Marriage so understood has been enshrined in American law. But viewed through the eyes of the Constitution, marriage is first and foremost a voluntary institution, shaped by individual choices. Protecting those choices is the top priority. It does not matter how recently the case for same-sex marriage has been advanced. The Constitutional principles invoked in support of it are immensely strong. So when the *Hollingsworth* and *Windsor* cases were decided, the Supreme Court did not hit a grand slam. But keep hitting home runs and you usually win the game, as *Obergefell* demonstrated. Under our Constitution, tradition is tradition but rights are trumps.

Prudence concedes the universalizing of gay marriage. Prudence also counsels that the new arrangements be given time to settle down. Now that same-sex marriage has been achieved, the spotlight will fade on the activists, and more sober assessments may begin. Everyone, including those who believe that heterosexual marriage is integral to the created order given by God, should be willing to ponder the potential benefits of gay marriage decisions.

Julia Stronks, professor of political science at Whitworth College, writes:

From a public justice perspective, [the *Hollingsworth* and *Windsor*] cases can be assessed in two different ways. Some will say that the cases emphasize what it means to do justice to same-sex couples, both in terms of legal recognition of their unions and in terms of protecting them from being targeted after they have secured certain rights. Others, however, will say that the cases failed to highlight the distinctiveness of marriage as an institution created by God. There is merit to both perspectives. This demonstrates that we have to think through two different things. First, we have to think about what it means to recognize a differentiation of institutions. Second, we have to consider what it means to do justice to different worldviews in understanding what the responsibilities of those institutions are.

There are decades of debate ahead of us. Thirty-seven states do not recognize same-sex marriage, and in those that do, it is unclear how governments will balance the rights of gay couples with the rights of other institutions like non-profits, churches, or schools that believe marriage is between a male and female. We have much work to do.[8]

These are wise words. Stronks puts her finger on a core issue. From the sphere sovereignty perspective outlined in chapters 3 and 4, both the "differentiation of institutions" and the impact of different world views for understanding those institutions come together. From that Christian perspective, marriage is a unique and irreplaceable institution, so its basic form, a covenant between a man and a woman, is vital to society's well-being. Government is no substitute for it, nor is an arrangement with lower levels of obligation. Committed same-sex relationships are no substitute either—not, it should be noted, against a common misconception of the views of Christians, because gay persons are somehow unable to love and nurture children, but because the contributions of father and mother are considered natural and necessary to the child's well-being.

But as Stronks points out, you can't stop there. You must consider how the liberty necessary to a pluralistic society should be taken into account. Religious or world view liberty is vital to a free society. In the public square, Christians may insist on the irreplaceable nature of heterosexual marriage for social well-being and their freedom to make that argument deserves the same protection as free speech anywhere. As a world view position, it is

---

8. Stronks, "Same Sex Marriage and the Continuing Conversation (2)."

entitled to full liberty. So, too, is the crusade for "marriage equality" a world view position.

If this were only a matter of two competing perspectives seeking a voice in the public square, defending the rights of both points of view would be a relatively easy matter. But clearly the supporters of each perspective wish to achieve more than that. Public law is at stake. Should the gay lobby be permitted to impose their world view on everyone else? Should Christians who support traditional views of marriage be permitted to impose theirs? If the "umpire" is our liberal tradition of individual rights and majority rule, then supporters of gay marriage have it in my estimation. Of course, umpires aren't supposed to have skin in the game! So the question emerges, how do you do justice to each perspective as one or the other is bound to emerge victorious? Can you do justice to both? Can the system itself be made sufficiently fair that citizens of all persuasions can affirm the fairness of the process?

If legal regulation of marriage must change in response to democratic debate, then it is all the more important that the medium of that change be a genuinely pluralistic process. The changes go further than the language of including same-sex couples implies. Marriage is being converted into a voluntary institution, whose commitments are provisional and whose connection to procreation and child-rearing is growing, legally speaking, thinner and thinner. I take issue with Stronks's characterization of diversity in this regard. She may not be right to imply that we are living in a genuinely *pluralistic* society after all. A better description recognizes America as a diverse society, but one governed by *individualistic* rules. The diversity of world views, religious and other, is evident. Its contribution to the ideological divide distorting political discourse has been the subject of an earlier chapter. What the American political culture lacks, however, are the norms or etiquette of genuinely pluralistic societies. Instead, the rules, to say nothing of the polarized parties, suggest a zero-sum battle to the death! But a genuinely pluralistic society seeks to do justice to the world view diversity represented in society in the ways that lawmakers are selected, and laws are enacted, implemented, and contested in court. A genuinely pluralistic society will also seek to do justice to the unique, complementary, and necessary roles that mothers and fathers play in the raising of children. Should either or both of these dimensions of principled pluralism be dismissed as a bigoted religious attempt to impose a world view on everyone else, then we should call for consistency and level the same charge against liberal individualism itself and the various positions it enables. Quite quickly, of course, it would become apparent that finding common ground is close to impossible.

The nearest I can come to a resolution that does justice to both perspectives—and others—in such a situation is this: Otherwise generally applicable laws should contain generous exemptions that protect the integrity of those with principled objections. Religious liberty ought to protect believers from taking actions that are forbidden by the teaching of the religion in question even if the law otherwise calls for them. A good example of what this might look like in practice is the dispute over the "contraception mandate" in the Affordable Care Act. As written, the law only exempted religious institutions that served largely their own members—who would hold the same views. Under pressure, the Obama administration broadened the exemptions to include religious colleges, but drew the line at businesses whose owners claimed the requirement to cover employees in this way violated their own religious consciences. The Supreme Court disagreed and upheld the right of owners of closely held businesses to be exempt from the mandate on religious liberty grounds.[9]

More often than not, the courts resolve these issues. America is notoriously litigious and Americans do seem to reach for their lawyers at every conceivable opportunity. Reaching genuine pluralism is going to invoke our adversarial legal procedures, I think. A better course would be for well-represented citizens to see more resolution at the legislative stage. All the same, the courts do reflect a responsive political system with a capacity to educate and to deliver due process. Even as the two sides argue a case, these procedures afford the opportunity to frame a single conversation and a broader common understanding. I think much more effort should be made to honor the adversarial process, however much one may fear losing. Few of the outcomes are quite as final as they may appear at the time. When the issues being litigated include those on which positions are taken conscientiously, appreciation of the adversarial process may never be more important.

But there is more. The adversarial process teaches a vital lesson for pluralistic societies. As Stanley Carlson-Thies of the Institutional Religious Freedom Alliance puts it, "[Pluralism] means not all individuals will consider themselves welcome in or well-served by every organization in our society."[10] His words deserve broad circulation. Pluralism does not imply harmony. It does not imply always reaching a common position and eliminating power

9. *Burwell v. Hobby Lobby Stores*, 2014.
10. Carlson-Thies, "Religious Freedom v. Civil Rights."

struggles. Genuine pluralism comes at a cost and it's a hard sell in an individualistic, polarized, and zero-sum culture where the expectation holds that the winner shall take all and that the loser must agree with him.

What might the future hold? As we discovered, there were just two years—not "decades—of debate ahead, at least as far as the conferring of marriage benefits to same-sex couples is concerned. The advocates' banner phrase, "marriage equality," proved to be a brilliant combination of two positive terms before which resistance has crumbled in the courts, the media, states' attorneys general, and among the general public. What may not be over, however, is the legislative response to the legal right. Let me explain.

If achieving legal recognition of same-sex marriages is the acme of the gay rights movement, then like other hard-won rights, the achievement actually opens up conversations that could not take place earlier. What do I mean? When the Supreme Court declared the right to bear arms to be a fundamental right under the second and fourteenth amendments, one of the principal objections to gun regulations was undercut. The standard objection held that any and every step toward regulation was simply a stealth move toward eliminating the right itself. Or take abortion. The history of abortion rights since *Roe v. Wade* has *not* been one of extension after extension of the right to an abortion—quite the reverse, in fact. A large number of regulations have been upheld in the courts, such that the right is now constitutionally conditioned by such requirements as parental notification, restrictions on late-term abortions, and more.[11] I submit that reasonable regulation is actually *easier* to achieve after an individual right has been declared and affirmed than before.

In time, the right to same-sex marriage, if its post-recognition fate resembles that of the rights to bear arms and procure abortions, may be accompanied by regulations pertaining to issues like public health, child welfare, and religious liberty. Religious groups are not the only ones concerned to protect the institution of marriage. Its health is important to government also. As we saw in chapter 4, government cannot effectively substitute itself for marriage. It steps in to provide remedial services, child welfare, legal services, health care, and education, all of which need to be paid for. When individual marriages collapse, these services will be called on to a greater extent. If the institution of marriage fades or is replaced by legal arrangements that lack the extensive obligations of marriage with

11. The seminal case testing these requirements is *Planned Parenthood v. Casey* (1992).

regard to child welfare, health care, inheritance, and education, government may find itself shouldering not only the substantial remedial burden but also some major responsibilities, however unsuited government may be to exercise those. More debate may *follow* legal recognition of same-sex marriage than *preceded* it.

Outside the political process, the advent of same-sex marriage may bring some new opportunities for the Christian community. Most Christians want to extend hospitality and fellowship to their neighbors irrespective of the question of same-sex attraction. Gay activists may have a vested interested in contradicting that claim, but it remains true nevertheless. However serious their misgivings about homosexuality, most Christians do not want to discriminate and do recognize how much struggle and, often, pain surrounds questions of sexuality in general, and same-sex attraction in particular.

Churches have tried with varying levels of success to make the case that Scripture's disapproval of homosexual activity does not imply a rejection of same-sex attracted persons. Gay civil marriage may give those efforts new hope by moving the conversation into fresh channels. Gay Christians in particular, but same-sex attracted persons in general, may consider that the civil arrangements give them a platform from which to re-engage the Christian community. The focus will no longer have to be on the securing of the right.

I can think of few better issues for Christians to take up with gay fellow believers than "how to balance the rights of gay couples with the rights of other institutions like non-profits, churches, or schools that believe marriage is between a male and female," as Stronks put it.[12] The balancing will ultimately need to be established in law and practiced in the conduct of public officials, so it is a vital conversation to be taken up in churches, too.

Conclusion

On both abortion and same-sex marriage, I have emphasized the actual and potential roles of government and have argued that Christian-pluralist perspective brings important resources to bear on resolution of these issues. On both issues, government's key responsibilities face distortion by the value priorities of the liberal political tradition. On both, the sheer heft

12. Stronks, "Same Sex Marriage and the Continuing Conversation (2)."

of that tradition does not encourage the view that a change of course is likely. But Christians cannot give up their efforts simply because this is so.

In the case of abortion, it has proven possible to advance responsible restrictions to existing abortion laws, and these, in concert with lobbying for substantial pregnancy care services, offer a positive path forwards.

The sheer novelty of same-sex marriage—fast wearing off—does not dictate a clear strategy and cautions against a hasty response at present, even though its future legal status as a constitutional right seems increasingly certain. Advocating respect for genuine pluralism, in both its structural and confessional dimensions, seems to be the right general strategy. It keeps government within its bounds. It pursues a civil political order where citizens learn to coexist with deep disagreements. But at the same time, getting there is going to involve suffering. Having broken free of its Protestant moorings, the liberal tradition now displays a tendency to treat its values as absolutes and to punish those who resist falling in line with them.

But then again, genuine, principled pluralism is worth suffering for. At its core, principled pluralism is a good thing—and a thing that Christianity should smile upon. The body of Christ itself is diverse, to say nothing of the wider cultures represented in society. Public justice demands that citizens' deepest beliefs receive respect in the public square.

Home and Abroad

Imaginative Resources for a Changing World

THE AIM OF THIS chapter is not to consider discrete policy issues, as the previous two chapters have done. Instead it will focus on resources in Christianity that may prove especially helpful for navigating the already troubled waters of this century in international relations and domestic politics—hence the title.

Christians bring unusual resources to bear on the political order: They already hold citizenship in another country. As "citizens of heaven," we are the people of God, "a holy nation," and a "royal priesthood," according to the First Letter of Peter (2:9). We are called out from the world, for the kingdom of God is "not of this world." Along with these declarations, the New Testament writers variously warn us not to conform to the standards of the world but to embrace the radical standards of the kingdom of God, the standards that reflect the central theme of this book that power is made perfect in weakness. In the fullness of time, even our "lowly bodies" will be "conformed to his glorious body" as St. Paul assured the church in Philippi (Phil 3:21).

For Christian citizens of the United States, or elsewhere, this alternative citizenship has considerable, and perhaps unexpected, utility. It liberates the Christian imagination to engage in just and compassionate policies and actions, sure as we can be by faith of the hope that is set before us. This citizenship is the basis, as St. Paul, the writers of the Gospels, and the author of the Letter to the Hebrews all remind us, for joyfully accepting persecution, the plundering of our possessions, even death, for the joy of eternal life—grounds for taking risks in the name of truth and justice. The New Testament writers encourage us not to hold tightly to earthly relations—families, possessions, even citizenship—and invite us into the new order represented by the hope of Christ's resurrection. Notice that this liberation does not encourage "world-flight," nor does it point to indifference to our world, our communities, and our families—quite the contrary. Love your enemies. Do good to those who harm you. Turn the other cheek. These are all modes of engaging with, not disengaging from, the communities we live in.

A transformation of Christian imagination may be viewed as part and parcel of the transformation brought about by a saving relationship with Jesus Christ—something good in and of itself. It has an added importance, however, in today's global environment. Such an imaginative transformation can be of profound help to Christians trying to navigate the mental, spiritual, political, and intercultural facets of a rapidly changing world.

Writing in 2007, James Skillen describes how the touchstone of globalization is the multiplication of relationships. Where once, "a few ambassadors and a few trading companies and, on occasion, a few armies made almost all the connections that existed among states," today, "hundreds of millions of people, many of whom represent millions of organizations . . . interact with one another across borders as quickly and thoroughly as they interact with people in their own countries."[1] Nation-states are no longer the traffic police for these myriads of interactions as in an earlier day. In fact, the sovereignty of nation-states is now shared with many other actors on the international scene, from multinational corporations to nongovernmental organizations (NGOs). Other governments or quasi-governments, some local, others *supra*-national—like the European Union or the World Trade Organization—now share the power that sovereign states once enjoyed almost alone.

Like many political cultures around the world, these developments have met with a mixed reception in the United States. Americans have strong traditions of independent activity in the world. In the republic's early decades, these took the form of isolationism, of President George Washington's aversion to entangling alliances with the colonial powers of France, Britain, and Spain. Today, isolation's younger relative is unilateralism, which flexed its muscle as the "Bush doctrine" as the United States attempted to respond to the terrorist attacks of 9/11/2001. That doctrine's watchwords were sovereignty, national security, preemption, and supremacy. With the largest military and the largest economy in the world, unilateralism has

1. Skillen, "Contending Ways of Life."

deep, sympathetic roots in American culture and looks to enjoy periodic resurgence in foreign policy for many years to come.

The "facts on the ground" will increasingly displace unilateralism as a viable approach to foreign affairs, however. As Skillen sees it, Americans must get used to the growing sets of initiatives shaping the world that are taken by other nations and groups, be it other monster economies like China's, or by multinational financial institutions outside the direct influence of the United States, wherever they may have their headquarters.

It is on this changing world of a billion new communicators that the resources of the body of Christ whose citizenship is in heaven come to bear. For those communicators are not confined to banks and companies but include religious organizations and the distinctive perspectives they share. Consider the Catholic Church. In a world that transcends the dealings of nation-state to nation-state, Roman Catholics, rich or poor and from widely different regions, share the same church, the same pope, worship in recognizably similar ways across national cultures, and pray to the same God, Father, Son, and Holy Spirit. Spiritual, educational, and material resources may flow with greater ease across national boundaries by virtue of these shared beliefs and the solidarity that they engender. As noted in many a denomination, the pattern of eighteenth- and nineteenth-century missionary activity typically saw missionaries traveling from the relatively developed world to the undeveloped world. Now the patterns are reversed. Smaller than the Catholic Church, but still global in its reach, the vast majority of the membership of the Anglican Communion, once an exclusively English church, are today found in the developing world, in Africa and Asia in particular.

In important respects, both the secular patterns of globalization and the religious resources of the imagination may have arrived in time to tackle issues that know no obvious boundaries. Scientific controversies aside, the phenomenon of climate volatility is global in reach, closely tied to the energy uses of rapidly developing nations whose patterns of supply and sales are also worldwide.

Skillen sees globalization putting fresh urgency behind old questions to which religion in general and Christianity in particular gives answers: what does it mean to be human? How may human creativity help the world? How does human sin contribute to crises that are harder to confine than they once were? What do human moral obligations look like in a world of ever more porous borders?

Religious traditions have well-developed approaches to questions like these. But these approaches now face competition that the more settled worlds gone by, worlds of empires secured by military might, or simply of national cultures safe behind poor communications, did not contemplate. World views are now all but universally available for "consumption," and thus they compete with one another. Some of these conflicts appear to be merely regional, such as the bloody clashes between Islamic and Christian communities in Nigeria, which have produce so many grim headlines in recent years. And yet, it is apparent that even these regional conflicts reflect, and are transcended by, an awareness of larger differences played out almost everywhere.

As we have seen in the historical relationship between Christianity and democracy in the United States, religion constitutes a particular species of world view, and world views have a tendency toward absolutism in the way they hold to truths about reality. Alongside traditional faiths in the global community we now find various perspectives with essentially similar features, which see the world through distinctive lenses and consider that their resulting recommendations wield authority. This holds true for environmentalism, capitalism, socialism, nationalism, and Islam, to name only some of the more prominent. Religion as world view is alive and well in the world, and more aware of itself in relation to competitors than ever before.

Thus Skillen conceives of "competing ways of life" as the most telling feature of the changing world of international interactions.

Against the insistence of advocates for a continued American military and economic hegemony, Dennis Hoover notes that some evangelical Christians, traditional supporters, have begun to distance themselves from facets of this approach. Public education, poverty relief, child labor reform, and prison reform are now likely to be on the agenda of many an evangelical, according to Hoover's research.[2] Modest though these developments are, they point to the beginnings of more imaginative Christian responses to the new reality, via initiatives that need not, and typically do not, sacrifice evangelical positions on personal moral issues.

It is Skillen's contention that the resources of Christianity are especially valuable for the advice they offer to the challenges we face. As he puts it, in our "shrinking, warming, flattening, warring world, people everywhere may legitimately ask, what does the Christian way of life have to offer by way of wisdom, justice, and love for the human responsibilities

2. See Hoover, "Evangelical Christians."

of governance, child raising, economic development, science, technology, schooling, and anything else that pertains to human life in this world."[3] The Kuyperian tradition on which I have drawn offers considerable guidance to flesh out the contribution that the Christian way of life may offer to the changing world. Its commitment to public justice, to the differentiation of the responsibilities of state and civil society—sphere sovereignty—and to the principled pluralism that seeks to enable societies to live with basic world view differences, has much to offer.

It is reasonable to ask, of course, what kind of organization(s) will be best suited to make this contribution. I anticipate not one, but multiple organizations. Christian Democracy has an international presence as far as organized political parties are concerned and these parties cooperate and exchange ideas. But the porousness of international boundaries permits quite modest organizations, like Christian churches, think tanks, missions organizations, and aid organizations, to communicate on a worldwide scale. The same is increasingly true of Christian universities, many of which offer online classes and whose residential classes are (slowly) becoming ever-more internationalized.

But in the last analysis, the enduring contribution Christians can make in the world lies in our transcendent citizenship in the body of Christ and our embrace of the power made perfect in weakness. What that citizenship may do is render provisional every other attachment. One thinks here of Jesus' hard saying, "'If you want to be my disciple, you must hate everyone else by comparison—your father and mother, wife and children, brothers and sisters—yes, even your own life. Otherwise, you cannot be my disciple'" (Luke 14:26 NLT). Seeking God's kingdom first is fundamental to the Christian way of life. And in the context of international political, cultural, social, and economic relations, it is a crucial value that allows us to surrender absolute or near-absolute allegiances of many kinds—to blood and soil and status in particular. If we take this obligation seriously in the international context, then our imaginations may help us toward just and compassionate relations of many kinds, both in the actions we take ourselves and in the initiatives we urge our elected representatives to pursue on our behalf.

3. Skillen, "Contending Ways of Life," 122.

A Home of Our Own: The American Case
for Christian Democracy

Ironically, the Christian imagination that can be fanned into flame by our citizenship in the kingdom of God and inspired by the realization of our membership in the worldwide body of Christ can find itself stifled here at home. For here, change is both less and more apparent. Our party politics seem mired in mutually exclusive and warring perspectives, each powerful enough to veto the other's plans yet not strong enough to prevail without offering major concessions to the other side. Both parties' postures are fueled by ideological and arrogant certainty. Low levels of citizen participation have not changed in a generation. Competitive districts are the exception, not the norm. We can still use the old terms and refer to democratic "discourse" but the reality is that both sides talk past each other and appeal chiefly to their respective "bases." Persuading opponents has given way to mobilizing supporters. Cross-party initiatives have not disappeared altogether—let's recall the "Gang of Eight" United States Senators who shepherded comprehensive immigration reform through the Senate in 2013—but are now likely to be remarked upon simply because of how rare they have become.

Paradoxically, the image of political sclerosis projected by partisan conflict is actually reinforced by the impression of the rumbling juggernaut of progressive social views, an impression of unstoppable change in a single direction. Lest it be thought that such concerns are the exclusive preserve of social conservative activists, consider again Hugh Heclo's assessment of the current state of relations between Christianity and democracy—his omnibus term for the American political tradition—in the United States. At the end of the work cited in chapter 1, Heclo concludes that separatism and "exit" are emerging again as viable strategies for Christians. Something very similar is found in the work of sociologist James Davison Hunter, who calls for a stance of faithful presence as the preferred alternative to the activism of the Religious Right.[4]

As one convinced that principled pluralism and its political expression as Christian democracy offers a better alternative than exit from the public square while expressing the faithful presence Hunter calls for, I wonder if the issue that needs to be revisited is the degree of independence necessary to action that is faithfully representative of a Christian point of view.

---

4. Hunter, *To Change the World.*

Over lunch a few years ago, an African colleague asked me why evangelical Christians in the United States had allowed themselves to be so firmly entrenched in Republican Party politics. Shouldn't evangelicals make their political positions known and demand that the political parties take those positions seriously if they want to earn the support of evangelicals?

Following Governor Romney's defeat in the 2012 presidential elections, evangelical entrenchment faced new questions, not from evangelicals but from other Republicans. *Red State* editor Erick Erickson reviewed a host of calls to throw social conservatives out of the party before defending their presence as a still-vital constituency. But the once unthinkable had been uttered.

Much of this grumbling may be discounted as the usual finger-pointing that follows an election defeat. But recent evidence from the Pew Forum and the Institute for Religion and Democracy lends it a paradoxical gravity.

In 2012, despite President Obama's success in winning many evangelicals to his side four years earlier, the faithful returned to the Republican fold. White evangelicals gave Governor Romney as much support as President Bush earned in 2004, while observant Catholics were almost equally emphatic in support of the former governor.

Paradoxically, the social conservatism reinforced by observant Catholics and white evangelicals is now associated with declining capacity to build winning majorities because the issues themselves no longer attract majority support. Does this signal a coming separation, even a divorce between these Christian groups and the Republican Party?

The calls for ousting social conservatives were not made against the background of electoral defeat alone, but also of the secularizing flavor of the 2012 elections. All of the three gay marriage ballot initiatives passed. Medical, and in three states recreational, use of marijuana won by heavy majorities, and in Massachusetts physician-assisted suicide only failed by a narrow margin. In the immediate aftermath of the Republicans' election defeat, a blame game was perhaps to be expected. It was never likely to succeed. But there is no time like the present for inviting a more sophisticated expression of social conservatism.

My colleague was surely half right. No party should take people's votes for granted. The preferred stance for Christians to take, on principled and prudential grounds, should resemble, I think, a kind of critical loyalty.

As we have seen, Democrats and Republicans embrace increasingly separated political visions. The two of them, however, remain rooted in a single tradition. That tradition, born of Protestantism and the Enlightenment, commits American governments to protect personal freedoms by a mixture of restraint, which safeguards civil liberties, and activity, which protects civil rights—essentially equal protection under the law. The agreement ends there. The big differences in American politics are strategic ones. From the key roles awarded to government and the individual have emerged mutually exclusive preferences for either state-based or market-based approaches to governing. Concerned to expand basic protections to citizens' economic and social circumstances, where a large measure of discrimination, danger, and deprivation affecting opportunity was to be found, progressives pressed for the construction of an American welfare state. By the mid-twentieth century, it was largely in place. Challenging the American tradition of limited government, the welfare state proved as expensive to maintain as its supporters considered its benefits valuable. Detractors now built the pre-industrial American model of limited government into a near-mythical set of psychological insights connecting individual initiative, responsibility, hard work, and societal prosperity, and sounded the alarm at the departure from these universal axioms. Where those who saw the welfare state as the ethical way forward championed government as the primary agent of transformation, the new conservatism championed the marketplace and sought to disentangle it from government in order to perform its no less morally steeped wonders—enhanced personal responsibility, accountability, self-reliance, thrift, and prosperity for all.

Both of these approaches, underwritten by the two major parties and cast as the mutually exclusive alternatives for American policy-making, disregard or belittle the role of civil society. Non-state and non-market institutions were and still are relegated to the margins.[5] They are not considered to be integral elements of public policy approaches or solutions.

Christians in the tradition of Abraham Kuyper, in which the Center for Public Justice works, regard civil society as a domain of differentiated human responsibilities, whose unique roles government should respect and accommodate—responsibilities no less weighty and significant for human

5. A critic might reasonably protest in defense of social conservatives that they do treat civil society seriously and that defense of "family values" has been staunch. I would argue that even the defense of "family values" sits uneasily in the philosophical setting created by the Republican Party, which is in almost every other respect aggressively individualistic. "Family values" is not an especially imaginative or broadly interpreted category, but a narrowly drawn one. It is, I would argue, much more obviously anti-abortion and anti-same-sex marriage than it is pro-family.

flourishing than those associated with governments or markets. This is the focus of the principle of sphere sovereignty. These diverse human responsibilities should not be reduced to mere market forces as if government power and market choice were the only options, the only frames within which to make policy. The "third way" represented by this Christian tradition would include recognizing the important role civil society institutions have to play in making human life fruitful. Without a robust civil society, neither government nor markets can make up the deficit. In important ways, a healthy government and a flourishing economy are dependent on healthy civil society, given that families, churches, commercial enterprises, charities, etc., shape the values and provide much of the "training" by which children learn how to conduct themselves, as adults, in those two domains.

A complementary dimension of this Christian tradition calls for principled pluralism, that is, a commitment to make space for the variety of world views found within society. Politically, that commitment is met not only by American-style religious freedoms but by going beyond these individual freedoms to ensure that government cooperates with, rather than contradicts, the expression of these freedoms in family life, education, health care, and the other facets of differentiated human caring.

Framing the Christian pluralist position as one committed to limited government and the cultivation of a robust civil society and a strong view of religious liberty over against the positions of both political parties on these matters, suggests that a posture of *critical loyalty* toward both parties is the most logically compelling Christian position. What do I mean by that phrase? I am trying to combine the respect and honor due to a political order that has sustained the rule of law and the blessings of liberty with the importance of speaking from a Christian perspective to the defects and injustices this political order displays. To combine the two attitudes is to create tension in one's own mind and community first and foremost. But they should be combined, not separated. Too often Christians in the United States have lurched between rabid criticism of the federal government and uncritical patriotic embrace of the system, especially when the latter can be held high above the political fray as "America," rather than checks and balances, Democrats and Republicans, taxes and foreign policy. To bring them together is to offer support and criticism from a position of engagement.

How close can or should this engagement be? That's where the history of the Religious Right has lessons to offer. Too close an alliance with any political party results in baggage one may not wish to carry. Certainly, you cannot expect the general public to differentiate carefully between the particular positions *your group* supports as a junior partner in a coalition and what the party stands for in general. People will associate you with the entire range of positions this party holds.

To put this a different way, the Kuyperian tradition does embrace important elements of social conservatism in respect for life and for natural institutions like marriage. But it goes further by committing government to public justice, not personal freedom, as its top priority. As I noted in the previous chapter, overturning *Roe v. Wade* would not exhaust government's responsibilities for supporting life. This tradition would go beyond social conservatism to require government to act to achieve public justice. Clearly, such a stance cannot be slotted neatly into contemporary liberal or conservative categories, so to avoid confusion—if for no other reason—a more independent posture makes good sense.

But in the absence of election rules that encourage multiple parties, independence for Christian perspectives cannot be articulated by forming a political party along the lines of mid-twentieth-century Christian Democracy—which would otherwise be the best of options in your author's opinion. Instead, then, independence for a Christian perspective will have to be sustained either by making prudential alliances and doing a lot of explaining or by refusing such alliances in favor of a think tank strategy of contributing to the political conversation in as even-handed a manner as possible. A think tank like The Center for Public Justice tries to do this.

Electoral Reform—A Long Shot for Justice

What about those election laws? In what I intend as both a compliment and a criticism, let me say that the United States has a "Model T" electoral system. As a leader in the mass-produced internal combustion automobile that a very wide swath of the American public could afford, the Model T amounted to a breakthrough technology. But in time, however beloved and cherished, it became outmoded. So, too, with our electoral system of single-member districts and a separate election in each. It's pretty antiquated. Almost all new democracies employ a different system. But through romanticism or inertia, we keep driving the same old rust bucket of a system.

If Christians wanted to get behind a movement for political reform—and political reform is always a long shot—let me suggest that it be a movement to replace the current system of elections to the House of

Representatives (or your state's legislature) with a system of proportional representation (PR). Proportional representation awards political parties the same percentage of seats in the legislature that they won as votes in the election. To do this, PR systems do not use our single-member districts but replace them with multi-member districts, or even at-large voting, where all the seats for a state or a province are awarded on the proportional formula. In a state like Maryland, for example, with ten seats, an at-large system would make sense. For California, with over fifty, several multi-member districts would work well.

How does PR work in practice? The reasoning is simple. Political groupings can represent many things: political philosophy, ethnicity, regional interests, or religious affiliations. In many cases, these interests will only attract the support of small percentages of the population of a state or province, let alone an entire nation. But that, of course, does not make them any less legitimate. They are comprised of citizens and citizens in democracies are entitled to representation. If the state is divided up into single-member districts based on population—as districts for the House of Representatives and state legislatures are drawn up—many a political group will find its supporters too thinly spread to win a majority in any given district. If they enjoy 10 percent support, for example, and that support is spread out evenly across ten districts, then their prospects of winning even a single seat will be close to zero.

Take that 10 percent as the percentage that would be won in a statewide election with all ten seats available, and proportional representation will award that group one seat. All of a sudden, organizing a political party makes sense for that group, despite its modest size. Voting for it makes sense, too. No longer need the candidate for the small party have to defend himself against a barrage of media questions asking if the party is diverting votes from the two main—what, more *legitimate*—parties. No longer need citizens who would prefer to vote for the small party worry about "wasting" their votes or worry about unintentionally electing an unattractive major party candidate.

So much for the mechanics. Why should Christians back PR? The simple answer is that here is a justice issue every bit as far-reaching as some of the more visible issues. Diversity may be the watchword of contemporary culture, but you would hardly know it by examining the political choices offered to citizens. Diversity alone, one could argue, implies something right about ensuring a range of political choices—a political system that would hold up a mirror to society. But diversity also adds a dimension of urgency to the issues of justice as stake here. The content of our diverse society has been described in many ways. Political scientist Clark Cochran and colleagues give prominence to the conflict between the ideal of an open society and the presence of strongly held moral values—which, when we think about it, echoes the tension between Christianity and democracy summarized in chapter 2.[6] Just as for international relations, the defining and certainly the most challenging feature of the politics of our domestic political culture is "competing ways of life."

Arranging the structures of political representation to reflect and respect diversity so defined is no easy task, but it is a vital one, if we are to respect basic human dignity. Some would say that the simplest way to do this is to extend constitutional protection to basic freedoms and moral convictions as private matters, and to distinguish sharply between private and public domains. Religiously inspired moral values belong in the private sphere, not the public square, they say. To a significant extent, this formula may be detected in Supreme Court decisions extending considerable protection to religious liberty (both individual and institutional) but restricting conscience-based liberty beyond this private domain.[7] But this won't do. The same citizens who hold traditional moral values also have the right to participate in shaping public policy, so they need to know that their views can contribute to the laws under which they must live, whether those laws reflect their views well or poorly. Similarly, the advocates of an open society need to know that, when laws determine the extent of religious conscience exemptions, they have been able to argue their position and to make their contributions to the law-making process.

A diverse society is best served by a principled pluralism that affords different world views the capacity for political representation. There has to be a reasonable possibility that a political organization can form and win seats. The mere theoretical possibility is not enough. A system of proportional representation does not force anyone to organize a political party. But it makes organization worth the effort. Winning just a few seats enables small parties to be represented, of course, and that's just the beginning.

6. Cochran et al., *American Public Policy.*

7. For example, in 2012 the Supreme Court, by a 9–0 vote, confirmed the "ministerial exemption" for religious hiring. But the Obama administration was most reluctant to allow exemptions from the contraception mandate in the Affordable Care Act beyond those applying to religious institutions and their own employees. The scope of such exemptions is currently under litigation before the high court.

Seats won translate into votes that can be traded in the legislature in support of policies favorable to the party. A small party can set conditions for supporting a larger one on certain issues.

Although multi-member districts were once more common than they are now, they were only ever employed in states with small numbers of seats where the proportional effects were muted. As long ago as 1967, however, when the federal Uniform Congressional District Act banned them for all states, only Hawaii and New Mexico still used them. The act reflects the concern that minority candidates would fare badly if they had to convince an entire state's population to vote for them. If minority candidates had to convince all the Republicans or all the Democrats in a state to support them, there may be a grain of truth to this concern. What the authors of the legislation appear not to have even contemplated was the organization of *new parties*. Many a potential party that would have no chance of winning if forced to contest a series of single-member districts could gather the 5 or 10 percent of votes necessary to win a seat if the entire state's seats were distributed on the basis of the percentage of the vote won by each party.

The ban on at-large districts is based on false logic. Worse, under the *existing* system redistricting can still work against minority candidates. The practice of "cracking" a minority population so that it is spread across several districts to weaken its potential influence can still be seen in many a redistricting plan.

Let's suppose PR is adopted and multiple parties of the kind I have described make their appearance. Wouldn't this create a society even more divided and divisive than American society presently is? I insist that this would not be the result! When you win a seat or seats at the "table" of decision-making, that achievement reinforces your membership in the community. You belong. Every political community expects, or should expect, disagreement. But when those who disagree are reliably included in decision-making, not excluded from it, their membership and legitimacy is reinforced. Justice has been done and disagreement, including the kind that results in political defeat, is much easier to swallow once membership status has been established.

Don't many parties produce gridlock by making it harder than ever to assemble majorities to pass legislation? The answer is that they do not as a rule because the common practice is for parties to make formal alliances with one another, called *coalitions*, which commit those parties to working and voting together. In parliamentary systems, small parties negotiate these agreements to ensure support for their policy positions. So the coalition system usually ensures that there is a governing majority and that legislation can be passed.

With just two parties and separation of powers, the American system is probably *more* vulnerable to gridlock than PR-based multiparty parliamentary systems. If PR were adopted in American House elections, it is highly likely that similar formal alliances would take hold all across the American system. PR would probably result in the growth of new parties over several electoral cycles, rather than occurring immediately after PR was adopted. Once these parties had become established, their visibility to the population as a whole would improve their chances of contesting senate and presidential elections successfully.

Prudential considerations raise their head at this point: PR remains a long shot. Working against it is the strong support for tradition that every culture displays. "We've always done it this way" has an emotional appeal. The most powerful forces ranged against electoral reform are the two major parties themselves. Remember that Democrats and Republican state legislators control the laws governing elections, including the drawing up of electoral boundaries and the forms of election that will be held. The fear of a change that could increase the other party's power, reduce their own, or encourage new competitors makes them innately conservative.

The case for proportional representation is one that Christians can get behind for several reasons. It is more representative of society's composition with respect to regional interests, ethnic interests, ideological perspectives, and religious viewpoints. Proportional representation systems elect higher levels of women to office than our current system does.[8] New democracies adopt it as a matter of course.

Crossing the Ideological Divide

PR may make an important contribution to crossing the ideological divide between Republicans and Democrats, a divide all the stronger for the way it reflects several overlapping fault lines: between active and limited government, between "Christianity and democracy," and between political forces artificially grouped by redistricting into ever "redder" and "bluer" districts.

An important goal of Christian political engagement is to offer the resources of the faith to the tasks that fall to government. Government,

8. See Dahl, *How Democratic is the American Constitution?*, appendix, table 5.

we recall, is concerned with seeking proximate, partial solutions for the issues that we confront in this world. In the earlier version of this work, Ronald Mahurin and I summarized those resources as a set of principles or values: social justice, respect for life, reconciliation, active compassion, wise stewardship, and empowerment.[9] What remains striking about these values is the way they defy easy categorization into conventional liberal and conservative categories. Christian Democrats hold to these values, but Christian Democrats' support of welfare state provisions is not incompatible with their equally firm support of free market principles for organizing economic life. Christian political engagement may require a larger degree of independence than the Religious Right-Republican alliance has displayed, and several decades of political experience since *Roe v. Wade* may have been teaching just that lesson.

"Offering the resources of the faith" may sound far too invitational and hospitable, to the point of naiveté even, to make a good fit with the rough-and-tumble world of politics. One imagines a cold shoulder more easily than an embrace! Traditionally, however, the practices that comprise such an offer include organizing political parties, setting up interest groups, lobbying for policy change, initiating lawsuits to challenge government action, research, and journalism. It is into this basic set of modes of engagement that questions of strategy, of best practices, if you like, should be asked.

Were Christian Democrat a meaningful party option in the US, its sheer distinctiveness as an alternative to both liberal and conservative options would reboot the political debate in what could be constructive ways, introducing fresh perspectives on justice and limited government.

In lieu of a political party, Christians should perform a cost-benefit analysis of all their current strategies. If direct political efforts are confined to organizing pressure groups and making common cause with a sympathetic political party, we should not forget that direct political action does not exhaust political influence. Citizens need to be educated well and it seems there is ample work for Christian schools, colleges, and think tanks to do. On the faith basis that even modest efforts done faithfully have their place, let us renew our commitment to these initiatives so that succeeding generations may find their imaginations fired by the good news and inspired to love and good works.

9. See Sherratt and Mahurin, *Saints as Citizens*. Those principles were originally drawn from the work of a cross-party initiative in the United Kingdom in the 1990s, the Movement for Christian Democracy.

Chapter 9 _____

Be the Church!

"Yours, O Lord, is the greatness, and the power, and the glory, and the victory, and the majesty: for everything in heaven and on earth is yours; yours is the kingdom, O Lord, and you are exalted as Head above all. All things come from you, O Lord, and of your own have we given you" (1 Chr 29:10–11,14 NASB).[1]

In the course of research for this book, I came across the following observation from political philosopher Sheldon Wolin: "The significance of Christian thought for the Western political tradition lies not so much in what it had to say about the political order but primarily in what it had to say about the religious order."[2]

This book opened with a series of questions about politics and government, most of them originally put to me by members of my church. It closes on a similar ecclesiastical note. May we draw an inference from Wolin's observation and say that *the most important thing Christians can do for a healthy politics is to cultivate healthy churches?* That declaration complements my emphasis on Christian hope, piety, and prudence as important foundations to our political reflections and actions. From hope, piety, and prudence may come an appreciation of the place of government in the fallen world. These biblical values should strengthen twin resolves: not to invest politics with the capacity to deliver final solutions, and not to flee the world either. These twin temptations are real enough. James Skillen once described them as "the drive to dominance" and the "flight to purity."[3] More

---

1. These verses are also used in the Anglican *Book of Common Prayer* as "offertory sentences" during the celebration of Holy Eucharist.

2. Wolin, *Politics and Vision*, 97.

3. Skillen, "Majority No Longer Moral?"

than this, recall N. T. Wright's insight discussed in chapter 3. However insignificant an initiative may seem, however unlikely to reverse corruption or break through political deadlock, all that is done in love, in obedience to Scripture, and in the power of the spirit, will be fulfilled in the coming kingdom of Christ.

You cannot be a "lone ranger" Christian, however hopeful, pious, and prudent. Fellowship and the discipline of church life are essential to the authentic faith that underwrites the view of politics I have presented. I view the invitation—it should be noted that the author of the Letter to the Hebrews makes it what we would call a "non-negotiable"[4]—to belong to churches and submit to their discipline as an every bit as urgent a call as the call for Christians to be more politically engaged. Arguably it is more important. The advice seems practical and far from mysterious. By meeting together we can encourage one another to "love and good works."

C. S. Lewis's Screwtape would be mightily impressed, I suspect, if apprentice devil Wormwood could show him that *he* had brought about today's fashionable resistance to organized religion among younger American Christians! Rejecting the institutional church brings with it a number of problems. It ensures that the diverse body of Christ will not know its diversity. If believers do not meet—old and young, parent and single, traditional and contemporary—then how will they avoid being confirmed in their prejudices? How will they obey God's call to worship, evangelism, care, and justice? How will they learn to recognize and speak the language of their brothers and sisters in Christ? How will they glimpse the global reach of the body of Christ? (There isn't really an app for that, is there?)

Scholarly research tells of a retreat from religion, especially organized religion, and of decreased willingness to make long-term, binding commitments. Sociologist Christian Smith has documented in detail the spiritual attitudes, beliefs, and practices of "emerging adults,"[5] also referred to as the "millennials." Smith's analysis reveals a generation of moral relativists, captured by consumerism, naïve about the power of sex, vulnerable to abuse of alcohol and drugs, and, despite optimism to the contrary, at least as socially and politically disengaged as earlier generations. But in perhaps the most important insight his research provides, Smith shows how these pathologies reflect the woes of the culture itself, which he finds as much responsible for

---

4. Heb 10:25.

5. See Smith et al., *Lost in Transition*. Emerging adults are eighteen to twenty-three-year-olds by the definition Smith and his colleagues employ.

the distressing outcomes he documents as the defective moral equipment and resulting poor choices of emerging adults themselves. That defective moral equipment results from moral confusion to a significant degree and from pervasive materialism in the culture. Together, these influences create only a confusing picture of what self and society ought to look like. As a result, Smith argues, "society itself is transformed, not into a rich network of various sorts of communities and social institutions that together comprise a civil society that promotes human flourishing, but rather into a national mega-supermarket of endless products and services where shoppers (having been 'empowered' by their incomes) seek human fulfillment through mass consumption." All this comes at a high price that surrenders "social identities, organic communities of solidarity, the civic virtues of duty and responsibility, and the learned processes of public deliberation, consensus building and conflict resolution."[6]

It is not hard to find in Smith's words an indictment of many a cultural institution, churches included. Human institutions show their weaknesses with very little prompting. Many of them have failed those whom they should be serving. But it is no less true that society may be much worse off if they fail altogether. Fellow sociologist Charles Murray, whose work was discussed in an earlier chapter, implicitly endorses Smith's observations about the wider culture. Murray detects a somewhat different kind of retreat from religion, one reflecting socioeconomic status, and not generational differences. Among America's poorer zip codes, institutions and the habits they engendered are in steep decline: marriage, work, religiosity, and respect for law.[7]

Sociologist Robert Putnam affirms Murray's findings. Concentrating on the arrested social mobility of millennials compared with their baby boomer parents, Putnam's study of Port Clinton, Ohio, in 1959 and 2009 documents the progressive closing off of opportunity to the later generation and the resulting polarization of "haves" and "have-nots" in today's America. Even the title carries the message. 1959's children really were "Our Kids" across wealth, class, gender, and, to a lesser but real extent, racial lines. 2009's children are segregated by wealth and related opportunity, Putnam shows, to the extent that the title description no longer even fits. In no meaningful way, he mourns, can Port Clinton's children claim that

6. Smith et al., *Lost in Transition*, 217. In particular, the discussion in chapter 5, from which the quotes are taken, is pertinent.

7. See Murray, *Coming Apart.*

status and the mix of affection, responsibility, and cherishing that once accompanied it.[8]

Reflecting the retreat from institutions, Steve Doughty, writing for Britain's *Daily Mail,* reported that Church of England congregations have fallen by half since the 1960s.[9] According to church statistics, only some 800,000 attend worship on an average Sunday. On a popular level, journalists on both sides of the Atlantic write regularly of innovations by leading clergy trying to reimagine or redesign people's encounter with the faith so that it does not resemble their parents' or grandparents' experience, in order to reverse these trends. Pubs, clubs, and cyberspace are now the sanctuaries of choice, were one to believe everything one reads, but what is missing from accounts of these new spaces and the initiatives that have brought them into existence is evidence that they are reversing the trends in attendance. But in fairness, perhaps the jury is still out on these initiatives.

The Sectarian Impulse

One common thread to popular and scholarly accounts of the aversion to institutions found among emerging adults may been termed the sectarian impulse.[10] I use that term because it gives these contemporary developments some history. They have happened before, with some predictability in the life of the church, since the earliest Christian communities were formed.

The earliest communities of Christians expected Jesus' return to be imminent. Under such circumstances, Christians probably bore a close emotional resemblance to Jews preparing for the flight out of Egypt: they were packed and ready to move. Plans were foreshortened, tasks were based on need not on rank, and as the New Testament describes the early church, the members "held all things in common."

As time passed and Jesus did not return as expected, a number of issues that had been relatively unimportant to disciples anticipating an imminent return rose to prominence. If sustaining the Christian community involved more than emergency preparation, but instead had to be directed

---

8. Putnam, *Our Kids.*

9. Doughty, "Just 800,000 worshipers attend a Church of England service on the average Sunday."

10. My point of departure for these paragraphs is the church-sect cycle. The concept originated in the work of sociologists and theologians of the early twentieth century, including Max Weber and Ernst Troeltsch.

toward long-term sustenance, then leadership, organization, and communication all had to be addressed. Indeed, as the generation of the apostles and other eyewitnesses died off, it became crucial to pass on Jesus' teachings in reliable fashion to the current and future generations. As church leaders fashioned the necessary means for doing so, Christian communities had to make changes. Who could be counted on as authoritative? How did one distinguish the authentic teachings from those that were heretical? To respond to questions like these, it was inevitable that more hierarchical structures had to be built.

Persecution rocked the early church, of course, but over time the church was able to enjoy some stability, all the more so once Christianity became the religion of the empire. Older tensions between the kinds of community Christianity and the pagan world represented weakened in the later years of the empire. Sheldon Wolin argues that this was because the Christians, with their well-developed sense of belonging to a community—the body of Christ with its high standards of honesty, probity, and service—could view the secular political order in two very different ways. When it persecuted the church, the Roman Empire represented the pagan world at its worst, at war with the community of the saints. However, when Rome faced its own dissolution in the face of barbarian incursions, Rome's stability, order, and lawfulness became much more attractive—and church leaders commended these features as virtues.

I think the same ambivalence may be detected in American Christians' ambivalence toward American culture. At war with it—in the "culture wars" sense—one minute, the next, we remain grateful for the stability and justice that our political order represents.

Criticism eventually arose inside the church as the relationship between church and state matured. Was the church not too cozy with the world, enjoying a privileged status and thus blunting its own radical edge? As the churches acquired institutional forms, so, too, Wolin says, did they acquire a view of time more suited to the life of self-perpetuating institutions than to the enthusiastic anticipation of Jesus' imminent return. On this level, too, the sectarians protested the distortion of the radical character of the faith. Politics had penetrated the church and the church had become accustomed to the priorities of politics. The church's egalitarian spirit was a casualty. What had happened to direct reliance upon God now that bishop predictably succeeded bishop and the fire of the Holy Spirit had been bottled up in the apostolic succession, where every bishop traced his lineage back to St. Peter?

In due course, groups of Christians acted on the sectarian impulse and broke away from "organized religion" to re-found authentic Christian community. This pattern was to mark the church over the succeeding centuries down to our own time.

Come forward a few centuries to the abuses in the Catholic Church that in part motivated the sectarian impulse we call the Reformation. Or consider the departure of Methodists from the Church of England in the mid 1700s, or the splintering into new denominations that has characterized American Christianity throughout the life of the republic. Come forward to the early twenty-first century where under the pressure of secularization and the decline of basic trust of others in society as a whole—not only in the church—there is a palpable scrambling to find ways to attract young people to, or back to, the church and to contain the departure of others.

These things have happened before, but in one important way, the contemporary pattern differs from what has happened in the past. Christians act on the sectarian impulse today because the church seems irrelevant to the culture, not because it has grown too close to it. Today's sectarians are willing to jettison anything that stands in the way of cultural relevance. Equipped as never before to customize their lives, millennials behave like yesterday's sectarians in their search for authenticity, but it is an authenticity that they want to "connect" in a positive, public relations manner, with the wider culture. So they discard buildings and institutional forms in the hope that by these actions they will display a culturally acceptable Christianity capable of attracting converts among the postmodern generations.

A. N. Wilson's wry observation about modern people and the heart of the Christian faith in chapter 4 warns that this familiar pattern of sectarian action is deeply flawed. After all, yesterday's sectarians rejected cultural trappings because these obscured or distorted Christian teachings and Christian community. Now what stands in the way of successful evangelism may be the very essence of the faith! As Wilson puts it, secularized people "just can't believe" in the virgin birth, miracles, and the rest. They naturally feel under no obligation to heed the church's moral advice either. So, how are they to be reached? Will meeting them where they are call for diluting the good news?

It is also telling that Smith's research found little support for the view that millennials in particular or their broader generational peers have developed alternative ways of connecting with the political process. Quite the contrary, it seems. Smith finds that the perception of greater social and political engagement on the part of the millennial generation is unsupported by evidence, and goes so far as to describe it as "sheer fiction."

All right, you may be thinking, what's your solution to all this? If churches are shrinking and even believers are rejecting institutions and "organized religion," how do you simultaneously stop churches from shrinking and hold onto authentic Christianity, which you keep saying involves really heavy lifting, you know, believing in miracles, and suffering for those impossible-to-believe beliefs? If churches are shrinking and churches hold the keys to fruitful social and political engagement for Christians, how can things be turned around?

Beyond the Sectarian Impulse

I have to say that the foolproof plan for righting the ship eludes me. I do think it's worth taking the historical tensions described above to the next step, however. The history of the Christian church shows that the sectarian impulse does not have the last word in the relationship between church and sect. Once they have broken away to set up their more authentic Christian fellowship, the sectarians discover for themselves that certain questions persist in ruffling the pure waters of sectarianism. Perhaps the break was undertaken to correct theological error? All right, someone will have to answer the question how theological purity is to be sustained beyond the current group of sectarians. What will new converts be asked to affirm? How and what will the next generation of church members be taught? Who will guard the authenticity of the faith? How are future leaders to be tested before assuming positions of leadership, or disciplined if they stray from the proper doctrine? If the sect broke away in the first place because the church seemed to be getting too comfortable with social norms, what sort of relations should now be established with society? How will evangelism be conducted?

Before very long, a new structure of rules and forms begins to emerge. In time, those forms and structures qualify the sect as more church-like—in all likelihood more hierarchical and less egalitarian than the sect aspired to be, and certainly more political. Eventually, conditions will be ripe for a new generation of sectarians to mount their familiar criticism of the way the church is run and what its priorities are.

I am skeptical of attempts to impose cycles of any kind on history, so I reject the notion that there is a predictable time frame to the wheel turning and the millennial generation embracing a more organized form of religion. What may be more important is for Christians to make sure that their churches reflect the radical character of the good news. We may disagree among one another how best to complement the radical character of the gospel by our organizational forms, but we need to keep that conversation going and we need to keep it saturated with love and respect for our brothers and sisters in Christ. There is too much at stake not to do this.

Christian Community, Politics, and Humility

Is the Christian community a superior community? Ouch! There's a question to bring down the forces of secular scorn on the church. We need to take it up, however. Is the Christian contribution to the good life chiefly one of pointing to the future, to the renewed and perfect community that will arise "when Christ shall come again in power and great glory"? Or does Christian community offer a more compelling form of society here and now, whose fruits can spread beyond its bounds?

The early church clearly thought it was the latter. Sheldon Wolin quotes the third-century theologian Origen contrasting the church in Athens with its city council, finding the former "quiet and steadfast," while the latter was "full of discord." He went on, "you have only to compare the ruler of the church in each city with the ruler of the people in the city, in order to see that . . . there is real superiority, a superiority in progress toward the attainment of virtue, when measured against the behavior and manners of the councilors and rulers who are to be found in these cities."[11]

We can see now at least one reason why Wolin thought that Christianity influenced political thinking not so much in the way Christians thought about politics as in the way they thought about religion. The church *was* a kind of polity and Christians were aware of this. Its power lay in its standards of conduct, its unity, and its willingness to recognize in its leadership a divinely ordained authority. Citizenship in the kingdom of God provided an essential perspective on citizenship in the fallen world. In the world, the Christian was an alien, a sojourner. One knew the true condition of the world that was made by God but fallen. Christian teaching told one to put the kingdom of God first.

11. Quoted in Wolin, *Politics and Vision*, 107.

The Psalmist expresses the kingdom perspective in Psalm 146. Let me quote it in full:

> [1] Praise the Lord.
>
> Praise the Lord, my soul.
>
> [2] I will praise the Lord all my life;
>
> I will sing praise to my God as long as I live.
>
> [3] Do not put your trust in princes,
>
> in human beings, who cannot save.
>
> [4] When their spirit departs, they return to the ground;
>
> on that very day their plans come to nothing.
>
> [5] Blessed are those whose help is the God of Jacob,
>
> whose hope is in the Lord their God.
>
> [6] He is the Maker of heaven and earth,
>
> the sea, and everything in them—
>
> he remains faithful forever.
>
> [7] He upholds the cause of the oppressed
>
> and gives food to the hungry.
>
> The Lord sets prisoners free,
>
> [8] the Lord gives sight to the blind,
>
> the Lord lifts up those who are bowed down,
>
> the Lord loves the righteous.
>
> [9] The Lord watches over the foreigner
>
> and sustains the fatherless and the widow,
>
> but he frustrates the ways of the wicked.
>
> [10] The Lord reigns forever,
>
> your God, O Zion, for all generations.
>
> Praise the Lord.
>
> (NIV)

Reading this psalm, Christians today will detect an echo of Origen's claims from many centuries later, but though convincing in principle, they may struggle to see the potential realized in our own churches. Today, churches seem more likely to echo the contentious Athenian assembly! I used to set my students an assignment designed to help them reflect on the sources of Christian attitudes to politics. I would ask them to plan an adult Sunday school class on politics for *their* home churches. The assignment was gratifyingly successful on that score. But I recall it chiefly for one stunning finding: invariably, when surveying the recent history of their typically Protestant churches, students would describe a split sometime in the previous one to three years. Some of these ruptures fitted the sectarian pattern described above, where the split was prompted by a quest for biblical purity, but most seemed to have happened for far less principled reasons. Instead they ran the gamut of personality conflicts, moral lapses, and other unoriginal sins.

Perhaps we should expect this. Perhaps Origen overlooked the natural consequences of successful evangelism! Jesus Christ draws the world to himself and as people respond to his invitation, they bring with them all of theirs and the world's troubles. So the church can rarely lay claim to superiority in the way it conducts its business or in the personal conduct of its members. Christians make countless mistakes in their personal and corporate lives. But what churches can, and must, do, however imperfectly they do it, is to witness to the hurting world's hope, Jesus Christ the risen King. It is the church's task to call this world to the next, to call the creation to its coming renewal.

In contrast to this broad remit of the churches, Christian *political* efforts address the tasks of the political order in *this* world, the world laboring under the effects of sin but pervaded by the grace, goodness, and glory of God. Christian political efforts attempt to enhance human flourishing in all its facets, mindful that political authority has to devote much of its energy to corrective work that falls to humans on account of sin—in other words, to the pursuit of the corrective kind of justice. Recall, from chapter 5, my insistence that the prudential tradition of Christian reflection is always relevant to our fallen world. In small ways or larger ones, each of us must learn the "balancing act" of bringing Christian principles to bear in circumstances of brokenness. The necessary emphasis on justice reflects the injustice in the world.

It would be a mistake, however, to say that the work of government— from the very mundane fixing of potholes, to raising the necessary revenue for transportation infrastructure, to scientific and medical research, to the hiring the police, prosecutors, public defenders, and judges, or to the work of diplomats and economists—is unconnected to the broader concerns of the church. The work of stewardship in the political arena does not come properly into focus, and may even become idolatrous in all the ways that the use of power does, without the perspective that the church teaches. The

Christian community loves the world, inspired by our hope in Christ, "who came to visit us in great humility," as the Anglican *Book of Common Prayer* has it.[12] The church preaches the good news of hope in Christ and the coming kingdom of God. Christian political efforts—whether in the guise of Christian Democracy, or the evangelicals' initiatives or the prudential tradition that warns against getting too close to democracy or any other system—seek inspiration and direction from the good news. But they do not, they should not, try to plant the kingdom of God on earth.

This point deserves emphasis: Christian political efforts all serve the created order and the challenges of life in society. They take their bearings from biblical understanding of what it means to be human. But they are not directed toward making the communities they serve into communities of faith. That task is the task of the church itself, which invites people into relationship with Jesus Christ. If the church is truly alive to the power made perfect, it will teach this distinction.

One of the reasons Christian political efforts could benefit from political party organization is that seeking votes among citizens further reinforces the distinction between the work of the churches and the tasks of Christians in politics. The democratic process helps Christian organizations communicate in an appropriate manner. To win elections, of course, you have to take your message to the electorate. You have to defend it against the competing claims of other parties. You have to articulate its virtues and acknowledge its limitations. Once in office, you (usually) have to share power. You have to concede others' contrary ideas in order to fashion legislation that will win the necessary approval. In all likelihood, your political fate will be connected, positively, to events you had little to do with, and negatively, to others for which you bear no responsibility. Success may meet with little reward, failure with permanent blame. All in all, democracy is a good school for teaching Christians humility on account of its frequent humiliations. Canvassing for electoral support among people who don't care about your faith commitment can keep one rooted in reality.

Churches and the Problem of Evil

The contributions democratic politics can make to foster a humble attitude in those who aspire to office, then, should not be overlooked. An even more basic rooting in reality begins with "'fessing up" to our own rebellious

12. *Book of Common Prayer*, "Collect for the First Sunday in Advent."

natures. And here it's the church that supplies the essential teaching. Reinhold Niebuhr put this as well as anyone when he wrote, "If the recognition of selfishness is prerequisite to the mitigation of its force and the diminution of its anti-social consequences in society, religion should be a dominant influence in the socialization of man; for religion is fruitful of the spirit of contrition."[13]

With these words, I want to underscore a defect in political systems from the democratic to the dictatorial. They pay too little attention to sin. None of them adequately address the problem of evil.

Beyond the insights of a Kuyper or the wisdom of the prudential tradition of Christian thought, it seems to me there is one resource Christians must attempt to convey to the Monday-to-Friday world of politics. They need to translate into plain language the reality of the problem of evil. As Niebuhr saw it in his day, secular political optimists name ignorance or irrationality as the villain at the center of the human condition. They offer, predictably, education and training in rationality as the needed antidotes.

For different reasons, democratic political discourse is also vulnerable to underestimating evil. First, it assigns pride of place to popular decision-making. Of course we consider this a virtue and, relatively speaking, it certainly is. But as a result, popular opinion or majority vote tends to monopolize the meaning of public good. This strong association evicts other meanings that compete with it. "Good" in democratic understanding may refer to more than majority rule—for example, deliberation is supposed to precede decision, so the majority that eventually decides a question becomes an informed majority—but it cannot contradict majority rule. So a good policy is one "We the People" have voted for. In a democracy, no alternative criterion for goodness is going to supplant it. Naturally enough, just as majority rule colonizes the idea of goodness, so evil loses its cosmic dimension of human rebellion against God, or, in more secularized terms, against a higher law. Instead, it becomes associated chiefly with actions or decisions that violate principles of majority rule!

The norms of democracy invite a second failing, directly related to the first. Democracy tempts us to imagine that *agreement can replace force.* Why is this? It is true that democracy has brought about considerable power sharing. The people's votes have replaced the whims, edicts, and commands of autocratic rulers. That, in theory, is an elemental sharing of power, a basic check on the pretensions of those who would govern. (All too often,

13. Niebuhr, *Moral Man and Immoral Society*, 51.

the people's votes are really echoes of the interest groups' efforts to lobby the political leaders and to massage public opinion.) But despite the imperfections of representation, it seems to follow that democracy can promise a force-free politics, where coercion has been replaced with agreements reached by free discussion. Power as force can be eliminated from politics! Except, of course, that it cannot. Once an agreement has been reached, once a bill has left the Congress to be signed into law by the President, it must be implemented. Its integrity can then only be upheld by penalties attached to disobedience—even if those penalties are not imposed except as a last resort. Some form of coercion must always remain, however representative the process adopted for enacting the law in the first place.

For those liberals or progressives who do attempt to take evil seriously, evil is named only when there is a need to underscore the heinous character of the offense. If personified, the tendency is to point to one of a handful of villains. This effectively places evil in a category beyond politics, converting it into a rare pathology populated by the few—Hitler, Stalin, Pol Pot, Idi Amin, and others. Sin's universal reach into every human heart can be easy to ignore when monsters like these paint it in such lurid colors.

Conversely, those influenced by the Marxist myth convert our universal rebellion as human beings into oppression of one class or classes by a ruling class, a perspective with just enough plausibility to sustain support for it. In the class struggle, the oppressed are innocent by contrast with their oppressors. So, here, too, the problem of evil is distorted and its scope unrecognized.

Can modern democracies, the United States' version among them, be persuaded to take the problem of evil seriously? Writing in 1950, only a few years after the close the Second World War, Christian political philosopher John Hallowell already worried that they were losing touch with it. "Modern man's great lack is lack of conviction, particularly the conviction that good and evil are real."[14] We need to get those words back and not give them up to rights talk or romantic hopes of replacing coercion with agreement, let alone to attractively packaged myths that lodge responsibility in some class of oppressors, anyone other than me. Where else but in the Christian community are we going to be able to nurture the language that "penetrates even to dividing soul and spirit, joints and marrow; it judges the thoughts and attitudes of the heart" (Heb 4:12)? Here, then, is a major task for the churches.

14. Hallowell, *Main Currents in Modern Political Thought*, 619.

Perhaps there is less danger than there was in the period Heclo characterized as the Great Denouement, that century and a half in which a separated Christianity and American democracy enjoyed a relationship of mutual respect. Even this desirable relationship, Heclo warned, was better for democracy than for Christianity. The fatal temptations Christianity succumbed to, in his opinion, include embracing democratic norms as if these expressed the faith, putting too much hope in majority rule, and embracing the myth of individual choice.

Christians should remind ourselves that we are absolutists, who give basic allegiance to a foreign power! Christian political initiatives must be grounded firmly in Christian teaching. The biblical narrative—creation, fall, redemption, judgment, and fulfillment—is vital to an authentically constructed Christian world view and to authentically Christian habits of the heart. Cultivating these is the task of the church.

Is There a Christian Politics for the Twenty-First Century?

It is time to sum up. The patient reader has been waiting for the author to answer his question. That question, in this book's subtitle, is a deceptively simple one, the answer not so simple. I have attempted to answer it in the way the book is structured. I compared the Religious Right with Christian Democracy as two major attempts to practice a Christian politics. Each left its mark and left us a record to peruse and reflect on. I then proceeded to ask what ought to be the elements of an authentic faith that could ground political engagement. I found these elements in Christians' hope in the coming of Christ. Jesus Christ turns politics on its head, setting radically new standards for conducting our business in this world. The power of God is perfected in weakness, Christ's weakness on Calvary of course, but also our own weakness as fallible humans made in God's image but following Christ. But this Christ is the one to be glorified as King over all. His way, the power he exerts, is equal to atoning for my sin. But it can accomplish more than that. The power made perfect in weakness defeats death itself. Its victory over evil will result in making all things new.

Christians' political engagement must not aim at domination, which would only collapse into idolatry, or at purity, which tends only to try to live apart from the world's struggles. Whatever form it takes, political engagement must try to conform to the standards set by Christ and should ground its efforts, large or small, in the hope of glory. To attempt to do so is to seek to please God—another dimension of authentic Christian faith that I argued must inform political engagement. No less important is the prudential dimension of political engagement. This reminds us of the modest scope of government and politics in the fallen world and of the need to avoid seeking ultimate solutions to its problems.

With these elements as a kind of composite Christian perspective, I considered three pairs of contemporary issues and argued that the perspective offers good guidance for addressing them.

In the present chapter, I closed with something of a plea for believers to recognize the irreplaceable role of churches—to come to a new appreciation of the church's importance. Only the churches, oriented as they are (or should be) to this world *and* the next can adequately foster the elements of authentic faith. Christians must belong to churches. We don't study and practice the faith in isolation. We are members of one another.

If there is a Christian politics for this century, then, its character depends more on the cultivation of the faith and rather less on the forms that political expression takes. The forms may be dictated by circumstances to a significant degree. It is important, as we saw in the perspective developed into Christian Democracy by Roman Catholics, and echoed in the sphere sovereignty of Abraham Kuyper, to explore how God's creation provides guidance for the role of government in relation to civil society. It is important, as the prudential approach affirms, to address politics in a fallen world with prudence and not in pursuit of ultimate solutions. It is important to approach politics with a determination that action be tied first to obeying God, in the tradition of Christian piety. But it is even more important to begin such explorations with the archetype of all rulers, elected and unelected, Jesus Christ. Christ is the rightful ruler who exercises power by dying for guilty humans. In Christ alone, power and love are one.

It is in keeping with these reflections to close with a prayer, or at least a call to prayer. The body of Christ, as some traditions prefer to name the Christian community, knows Christ as King, expects Christ to return in glory to rule with his suffering love, holds out as its hope our resurrection with renewed bodies and the reconciliation of all things, seeks the lost, longs for the way of peace, and prays that we be "godly and quietly governed." That latter lovely expression from the Anglican *Book of Common Prayer* echoes St. Paul's words to Timothy. I find in them not only an appropriate prayer for those who hold political office but also an appropriate context for the importance of government, and thus an echo of the focus of this book:

> First of all, then, I urge that petitions, prayers, intercessions, and thanksgivings be made for everyone, for kings and all those who are in authority, so that we may lead a tranquil and quiet life in all godliness and dignity. This is good, and it pleased God our Savior, who wants everyone to be saved and to come the knowledge of the truth. For there is one God and one mediator between God and humanity, Christ Jesus, Himself human, who gave himself—a ransom for all, a testimony at the proper time (1 Timothy 2:1–6 HCSB).

Amen to that!

Bibliography

Balmer, Randall. "The Real Origins of the Religious Right." www.politico.com/magazine/story/2014/05/religious-right-real-origins-107133.html#ixzz331HdcNWA.

Black, Amy E. *Honoring God in Red or Blue: Approaching Politics with Humility, Grace, and Reason.* Chicago: Moody, 2012.

Boffetti, Jason. *All Schools are Public Schools: A Case for State Aid to Private Education and Homeschooling Parents.* Washington, DC: Faith and Reason Institute, 2001.

The Book of Common Prayer. www.bcponline.org.

Carlson-Thies, Stanley. "Religious Freedom v. Civil Rights. *Capital Commentary,* December 6, 2013. http://www.cpjustice.org/public/capital_commentary/article/245.

Cary, Noel D. *The Path to Christian Democracy: German Catholics and the Party System from Windthorst to Adenauer.* Cambridge, MA: Harvard University Press, 1996.

Cochran, Clark E., et al. *American Public Policy: An Introduction.* 10th ed. Boston: Wadsworth, Cengage Learning, 2011.

Dahl, Robert A. *How Democratic is the American Constitution?* New Haven, CT: Yale University Press, 2001.

Dickinson, Emily. "Tell all the truth but tell it slant." In *The Poems of Emily Dickinson: Reading Edition,* edited by Ralph W. Franklin, 494. Cambridge, MA: Belknap, 1998.

Doughty, Steve. "Just 800,000 worshipers attend a Church of England service on the average Sunday." *Daily Mail,* March 21, 2014.

Eliot, T. S. *Four Quartets.* New York: Harcourt, Brace, 1964.

Fogarty, Michael. *Motorways Merge: The New Challenge to Christian Democracy.* Ware, Hertforshire: Christian Democrat Press, 1999.

Gushee, David. *The Future of Faith in American Politics: The Public Witness of the Evangelical Center.* Waco, TX: Baylor University Press, 2008.

Hallie, Phillip. *Lest Innocent Blood be Shed: The Story of the Village of Le Chambon and How Goodness Happened There.* New York: Harper Perennial, 1994.

Hallowell, John H. *Main Currents in Modern Political Thought.* 1950. Reprint. Lanham, MD: University Press of America, 1985.

Heclo, Hugh. *Christianity and American Democracy.* Cambridge, MA: Harvard, 2007.

Hoover, Dennis R. "Evangelical Christians: The New Internationalists?" In *Prospects and Ambiguities of Globalization,* edited by in James W. Skillen, 93–106. Lanham, MD: Lexington, 2009.

Howe, Amy. "A Home Run but Not a Grand Slam for Gay Marriage." http://www. scotusblog.com/2013/06/a-home-run-but-not-a-grand-slam-for-gay-marriage-advocates-in-plain-english/.

Hunter, James Davison. *To Change the World: The Irony, Tragedy and Possibility of Christianity in the Late Modern World.* New York: Oxford University Press, 2010.

Jenkins, Philip. *The Next Christendom: The Coming of Global Christianity.* 3rd ed. New York: Oxford University Press, 2011.

Johnson, James Turner. "Just War, as it was and is." *First Things* 149 (2005) 14–24.

Kraynak, Robert P. *Christian Faith and Modern Democracy: God and Politics in the Fallen World.* Notre Dame, IN: University of Notre Dame Press, 2001.

Kuyper, Abraham. "The Anti-Revolutionary Program." In *Political Order and the Plural Structure of Society*, edited by James W. Skillen and Rockne M. McCarthy, 235–64. Grand Rapids: Eerdmans, 1991.

———. *Calvinism: Six Stone Foundation Lectures.* Grand Rapids: Eerdmans, 1943.

———. *Sphere Sovereignty.* Kampen: J. H. Kok, 1930.

Mann, Thomas, and Norman Ornstein. *It's Even Worse Than It Looks.* New York: Basic, 2012.

McClain, Linda. "Unleashing or Harnessing 'Armies of Compassion'?: Reflections on the Faith-Based Initiative." *Loyola University Chicago Law Journal* 361 (2008) 361–426.

Minogue, Kenneth. *Politics: A Very Short Introduction.* Oxford: Oxford University Press, 1995.

Murray, Charles. *Coming Apart: The State of White America, 1960–2010.* New York: Random House, 2012.

Niebuhr, Reinhold. *An Interpretation of Christian Ethics.* New York: Meridian, 1956.

———. *Moral Man and Immoral Society.* New York: Scribner's, 1960.

O'Driscoll, Cian. "James Turner Johnson's Just War Idea: Commanding the Headwaters of Tradition." *Journal of International Political Theory* 4:2 (2008) 189–211.

Page, Benjamin I. *Choices and Echoes in Presidential Elections: Rational Man and Electoral Democracy.* Chicago: University of Chicago Press, 1979.

Putnam, Robert D. *Our Kids: The American Dream in Crisis.* New York: Simon and Schuster, 2015.

Schulzke, Erik. "Supreme Court upends marriage debate." *Deseret News*, June 26, 2013.

Sherratt, Timothy. "Christian Democracy in America?" In *Christianity and Civil Society*, edited by Jeanne Heffernan Schindler, 137–63. Lanham, MD: Lexington Books, 2008.

———. "No Ultimate Political Solutions." *Capital Commentary*, October 18, 2013. http://www.cpjustice.org/public/capital_commentary/article/269.

———. "Religion, Abortion and the Role of Government." *Capital Commentary*, October 19, 2012. http://wwe.cpjustice.org/public/capital_commentary/474.

———. "Same-Sex Marriage and the Power of Rights." *Faith + Ideas =*, Gordon College, Wenham, MA, July 9, 2013.

———. "Simply Because It's the Right Thing To Do." *Capital Commentary*, April 4, 2014. http://www.cpjustice.org/public/capital_commentary/181.

Sherratt, Timothy, and Ronald P. Mahurin. *Saints as Citizens: A Guide to Public Responsibilities for Christians.* Grand Rapids: Baker, 1995.

Skillen, James W. "Contending Ways of Life." In *Prospects and Ambiguities of Globalization: Critical Assessment at a Time of Growing Turmoil*, edited by James W. Skillen, 107–24. Lanham, MD: Lexington, 2007.

———. *In Pursuit of Justice: Christian-Democratic Explorations*. Lanham, MD: Lexington, 2004.

———. "Majority No Longer Moral?" *Capital Commentary*, March 15, 1999. http://wwwcpjustice.org/public/capital_commentary/article/1202.

Smith, Christian, et al. *Lost in Transition: The Dark Side of Emerging Adulthood*. New York: Oxford University Press, 2011.

Stronks, Julia. "Same Sex Marriage and the Continuing Conversation (2)." *Capital Commentary*, July 5, 2013. http://www.cpjustice.org/public/capital_commentary/article/329.

United States Conference of Catholic Bishops. "Supreme Court decisions on Marriage: Tragic Day for Marriage and Our Nation State U.S. Bishops." www.usccb.org/news/2013/13-126.cfm.

Van Kersbergen, Kees. "The Distinctiveness of Christian Democracy." In *Christian Democracy in Europe: A Comparative Perspective*, edited by David L. Hanley, 31–47. London: Pinter, 1994.

Wang, Stephanie. "Indiana voucher students double to nearly 20,000." *Indianapolis Star*, January 27, 2014.

Williams, Charles. *Adenauer: The Father of the New Germany*. New York: John Wiley & Sons, 2000.

Williams, Mari. "Surprised by Tom Wright: How 'Surprised by Hope' is changing my whole outlook on life and death." http://resistanceandrenewal.net/2012/06/27/surprised-by-tom-wright-how-surprised-by-hope-is-changing-my-whole-outlook-on-life-and-death-by-mari-williams/.

Wilson, A. N. "Lord Carey's Vision for the Church Might Kill It Off." *Daily Telegraph*, November 19, 2013. www.telegraph.co.uk/news/religion.

Wolin, Sheldon S. *Politics and Vision*. Boston: Little, Brown, 1960.

Wright, Christopher J. H. *Living as the People of God*. Downers Grove, IL: InterVarsity, 1984.

Wright, N. T. *How God Became King: The Forgotten Story of the Gospels*. New York: HarperOne, 2012.

———. "Keep the Faith." June 22, 2015. http://www.spectator.co.uk/essays/7174863/keep-the-faith.html.

———. *Surprised by Hope*. New York: HarperCollins, 2008.

Index

Index

Made in the USA
Coppell, TX
03 January 2021

47502694R00090